A Temporary European

The Adventures Of An American TV Reporter On the Continent

Walt Christophersen

Copyright 2009 by Walt Christophersen

2016 Edition

All rights reserved. No part of this publication may be reproduced, stored in a retrieval system or transmitted in any form or by any means, electronic, mechanical, photocopying, recording or otherwise, without prior written permission of the author, except by a reviewer who may quote brief passages.

ISBN 978-0-615-32092-2

Cover:
Photo by Rick Gayle, Phoenix
Pictured (l-r): Radio Free Europe ID
             Deutsche Welle ID
             International press pass

Map courtesy of Michelin North America, Inc.
All rights reserved.

Back cover portrait by David Schmidt, Phoenix

Also by Walt Christophersen:
By Ship, Train, Bus, Plane & Sometimes Hitchhiking

Buckeroo Books
Arizona USA
E-mail: eurobook@q.com

Contents

Living like a European   1
The show must go on • Up in the mornin' and off to school • *Die Deutsche Welle* • The right place at the right time • A lift to Cologne • Introducing Rex and Rendy • New meaning to the word elegant • At last, an apartment • Shooting the *Deutsche Welle* way • The Americanization of *EJ* • Storing the dog • Buying wheels • The Neanderthal incident • On the job • Legoland, the Pied Piper and gingerbread cookies • D-Day +40 • Holding hands in Verdun • Dresden +40 • The last POWs • The wall • The smile of espionage • Police, police! • The flood

Adjustments   65
Shopping, European style • What's in a name? • A new word: *Vorschuß* • *Krankenversicherung* • Income tax or *Lohnsteuer* • Writing wrongs • *Urlaub*

Interlude   75
Pause • *La catastrophe* • Land of curiosities • Paris

Back on the staff   89
Act II at the *DW* • Another new face • Return to Iceland • The last lonely Nazi • The more things change … • Strangest interview • Tapestry • Three degrees of separation • Jacques Brel lives on • Sherlock Holmes • Go West • One thing leads to another • Cyprus • The beloved 2CV • Four-legged friends • Travels with Mr. Sluggo • Further travels with Warras • Less traveled roads

Gyrations   143
Under new management • Back to the USA • The dreaded writing test & a bizarre interview • Quake! • Fighting back • Another shot at Cologne • Beautiful Blue Danube • *EJ* slips away • Surprise, you're hired • Getting down to work • The unfortunate demise of Mr. Sluggo • Introducing Mr. Dog • A solid offer • Finally hired • The unraveling • This … is CNN • Red-Eye to Berlin • Jumping to CNNI • Berlin epilogue

Living like a European

The show must go on

We were in Paris doing an interview with a wine expert about the *Beaujolais Nouveau*.

My German camera crew and I had already been in Burgundy shooting the vineyards, the bottling plant and the trucks rolling out at midnight in a heavy rain to deliver the first cases of the new wine. We were finishing up with a spokesman from the wine industry who was going to tell us what a great vintage it was.

As the crew was setting up the lights and camera in the second floor conference room, the spokesman, a well-dressed older man with white hair, sat at a huge conference table typing background material for me, pecking away with two fingers. After he finished, he said he was going to make copies. He walked across the room and headed down the stairs.

Seconds later, I heard strange thumping sounds as if someone had dropped something heavy, but I didn't think anything of it.

It soon became clear that the noise had been the man falling down the stairs. When he returned – clutching the copies – he was bleeding from the right corner of his forehead. The knuckles on one of his hands were badly scuffed. A woman carrying a bottle of hydrogen peroxide and a large bag of cotton balls rushed to catch up with him. She dabbed at his forehead as he sat down.

I immediately said, "Forget the interview. It's not important. Go see a doctor!"

But he insisted. I moved my chair a little to one side so he would turn his head, decreasing the chance that the camera would see the glistening bruise. Then we did it – one of the quickest interviews ever. All I was thinking of was finishing as soon as possible so he could get medical attention.

You never know what you'll run into when you set out to shoot a story. Maybe someone who's reluctant to talk. Maybe someone who's determined to complete the interview no matter what.

Up in the mornin' and off to school

My introduction to living and working in Europe began in 1983 in Kassel, a clean, pleasant city in the center of Germany with a population of nearly 200,000. Its main claim to fame was that Jakob and Wilhelm Grimm, the brothers who wrote the fairy tales, had lived there in the early 1800s.

After years of going to an office, I was setting off for school each morning carrying my books and papers in a canvas bag slung over my shoulder. It was September. The weather was sunny and pleasant. I left the house, walked downhill a couple of blocks, then hopped onto the *Strassenbahn* (streetcar) and rode downtown.

The school was *Europa Kolleg,* a private school for anyone who wanted to learn German. I was enrolled in an intensive one-month course in preparation for my new job with German broadcasting in Cologne.

There were dozens of students from all over the world in a wide range of ages, with most in their 20s.

On the first day, they sat us down at long folding tables in the gymnasium to take a placement test. Afterward I was told I did well enough to be put in an intermediate class. I protested, saying I knew almost no German and just got lucky because the test was multiple choice.

I'd been in Germany many years before, hitchhiking and staying in youth hostels, but the only thing I knew was sentences such as, *"Wo ist der Bahnhof?"* (Where is the train station?) The administrators believed me and placed me with the beginners.

The language course was a package deal that included lodging with a German family. In my case, it was the Plössers: a quiet lawyer in his 40s, his buxom, always cheerful 30-something wife, their son Marcus, who was in elementary school, and their dog, a drooling boxer named Boris.

I never did know the couple's first names because adults in Germany are generally introduced as Herr or Frau so-and-so, with first names rarely mentioned.

When I first arrived, Frau Plösser picked me up at the train station where I had grabbed a beer while trying to shake off a bad case of jet lag. I had flown from Kansas City via Chicago to Frankfurt, then rode the train for a few hours to Kassel.

When I changed planes in Chicago, my flight arrived late and I had to run through the sprawling terminal to the Lufthansa check-in. Even though I was sweating, panting and apologizing, the Lufthansa lady pounded the counter and said, "You must be here at least one hour before departure!" An early introduction to Germany.

The Plössers lived in a magnificent three-story mansion, putting them in a class far above a typical German family. Their house overlooked the city from an old neighborhood on the edge of an 865-acre park that was the biggest attraction in town. Inside the park, which dated from 1701, was an old castle housing an art museum plus an enormous statue of Hercules – a symbol of the city – that towered over a cascading waterfall.

I had my own room with private bath on the top, or third, floor. Another student, a French woman, had a room on the second floor. That's second floor American style. In Europe, the second floor is called the first floor because the first floor is known as the ground floor.

The Plössers obviously weren't taking in students to pick up extra money. They said they did it because they enjoyed meeting people from all over the world. In fact, they had a scrapbook filled with photos of their many guests.

The host families were supposed to speak only German so we could learn faster. The Plössers did so with the French woman because she was more advanced. But with me, they relented and spoke English. After all, it's difficult to carry on a conversation over lunch when the only things you know come from Chapter One, such as, *"Herr Fischer ist Flugkapitän."* (Mr. Fischer is an airline captain.) and *"Frau Berg ist Verkäuferin."* (Mrs. Berg is a cashier.)

Actually, Frau Plösser did teach me a few phrases. Each morning she would ask, *"Haben Sie gut geschlafen?"*

It didn't take long to figure out she was asking if I had slept well.

Those two dots over the "o" in Plösser and the second "a" in *Flugkapitän* are called umlauts. An umlaut is also used over the vowel "u" as in München. They indicate the presence of an unprinted "e" after the vowel, which of course renders the word unpronounceable for anyone but a German.

One of the first things I learned about Germany was that the midday meal is often the main meal of the day. School ran from 8 a.m. until one in the afternoon. After the French woman and I got home, usually traveling separately, we joined our hosts on the patio behind the house, sitting around an umbrella-shaded table. On the first day, I thought the meal was a bit extravagant for lunch. I was right. With a main course, salad and dessert, that was as good as it got.

Germans didn't seem to worry about cholesterol. The standard evening meal turned out to be an assortment of bread, cheese and sausage left next to the slicing machine in the kitchen. It was tasty and convenient.

Another thing I soon became aware of was that I seemed to have a fetish for cleanliness compared with my hosts. After the first week, Frau Plösser asked if she could take care of my laundry. I said sure and gave it to her. The next day I went down to the basement to retrieve my clothes, which were hanging from lines in a room set aside for drying. I was surprised to find I had run through as much clothing as the entire family. After that, I secretly washed most of my underwear and socks in my room to avoid embarrassment.

I later discovered that washing as few clothes as the Plössers did was not typical in Germany.

Learning German proved to be difficult despite the fact that we had a class of only seven. The other students were a woman from Mexico and an American engineering professor, both in their thirties, a petite teenaged Italian girl and three young Frenchmen.

As far as ability went, I ranked in the middle along with the Mexican woman. She worked for her national airline and was learning the language so she could converse with German passengers.

The smartest students were the professor, who was headed for a temporary teaching job in Germany, and the Italian girl. She lived in Luxembourg where her father was a diplomat. She could already speak English and French and had studied Greek and Latin, so she kept complaining about how easy the class was.

Those two obviously had the advantage of being more accustomed to a learning situation than the rest of us. Besides, the professor said the woman he was staying with refused to speak English.

At the other end of the scale were the Frenchmen. They were construction workers who were preparing to attend a school in Cologne that taught old-fashioned techniques for masonry, carpentry, bricklaying, roofing and similar trades. Those skills were still in demand for repairing old buildings or reproducing an old look in new buildings.

One of the teachers stressed telling time the German way, saying, *"Nicht digital!"* if we screwed up. For example, we shouldn't say "Two thirty." Make it "Half three" (*Halb drei*). Not "Two forty-five" but "A quarter to three" (*Viertal vor drei*). "Twenty past two" (*Zwanzig nach zwei*) rather than

"Two twenty." Etc.

The teachers told us the most perfect German in the country was spoken in the Hannover area to the north. *Hochdeutsch* they called it, meaning high German. There are many dialects in Germany and they're so different that a person from the southern state of Bavaria might have trouble conversing with someone from Friesenland, along the north coast, unless he used *Hochdeutsch*.

Even in proper German, there are regional differences. For instance, what we know as a hard dinner roll is called a *Brotchen* (little bread) in Cologne and a *Semmel* in Bavaria.

The Bavarians, along with the German-speaking Swiss and Austrians, have a sing-song accent that is sometimes ridiculed by the Germans in the center of the country who view them as country bumpkins.

I didn't realize it when I was there but the school was quite good. Although we spent most of the time working on grammar, one hour each day was devoted to the *Sprachlabor* (speech laboratory) where we were drilled on pronunciation.

One thing the teachers stressed was that we should memorize the gender of each word, whether it was *der, die* or *das,* male, female or neutral. For example, there are two words for car: *Auto* and *Wagen*. And it's *das Auto* and *der Wagen*. (Nouns are capitalized in German.) Gender affects the construction of the entire sentence, so knowing it is of critical importance. Memorization is the only way to do it.

We had plenty of homework, called *Hausaufgaben*, and surprise tests to keep us on our toes. There was even a written and oral final exam that was pretty tough. For the oral quiz, I stumbled through a statement about my dog, Mr. Sluggo, who was in the care of my father until I got settled in Cologne.

At the end, the Frenchmen had learned little more than the common German phrases: *Alles klar?* (Everything clear?) And the response: *Kein problem.* (No problem.)

When the diplomas were handed out, each said so-and-so "has completed the course," followed by a blank space where additional words could be written in by hand.

The professor and the Italian girl got diplomas that said "has completed the course with great success."

The Mexican woman and I received diplomas that said "has completed the course with success."

The Frenchmen were handed diplomas that said simply "has completed the course."

Die Deutsche Welle

I was to be working at the *Deutsche Welle*, a worldwide broadcast operation similar to the Voice of America and the BBC World Service. The *Welle,* as the people who worked there sometimes called it, sent out radio programs in German and 33 other languages. It had also branched out into television, producing sports and current affairs shows, mostly for third world countries.

Translated into English, *Deutsche Welle* literally means German Wave. It's pronounced doy-cha vehl-ah.

The program I was joining was *European Journal*, a weekly TV newsmagazine broadcast on about 160 PBS stations in the United States as well as some outlets in Canada and Australia.

The idea behind the program was brilliant. Although it featured stories from all over Europe, it was intended as a subtle way of informing viewers about Germany. Sort of, "If you know us, you'll like us." Officials in the capital, Bonn, who reviewed every script, apparently realized that a program perceived to be solely about Germany wouldn't attract as many viewers as a show covering all of Europe. But there was no attempt to hide the fact that the program came from

Germany and there didn't seem to be a quota for German stories. An announcement at the beginning said it was produced in Cologne and was partly sponsored by Lufthansa.

The right place at the right time

Getting the job was an amazing bit of good luck. I had been living in Columbus, Ohio and was looking for work following a nightmarish experience as a TV news director. I was hoping to steer clear of management and get a job as a reporter.

One of the resources I used was a relatively obscure job bulletin published by the Radio-Television News Directors Association. It came out twice a month and the usual subscription consisted of four issues. I subscribed only once and one of the issues just happened to list the job. If I hadn't subscribed at precisely that time, there's no way I ever would have known about it. The notice said:

> FIELD REPORTER. For Transtel, Cologne, West Germany. Experience in producing/editing for "EUROPEAN JOURNAL" (weekly news magazine distributed in the U.S.). Minimum two years experience. Background in European affairs and culture. Strong research, interviewing, reporting, writing and editing skills. Working knowledge of German and/or willingness to participate in four-week intensive language course in Germany prior to start of work.

Technically my employer was European Television Service, an independent company operating within the *Deutsche Welle*. Transtel, the firm cited in the ad, was its distribution arm. But for all practical purposes, I worked for the *Welle*.

A Temporary European

The notice went on to tell interested applicants to send their audition tape and resumé to Dr. Christian P. Stehr, a German language professor at Oregon State University in Corvallis who served as Transtel's U.S. representative. After I sent my tape, he mailed me a copy of one of their shows. It had stories from all over Europe including the Mediterranean island of Malta. I watched it thinking, "Oh boy! Doing stories in Malta. Wow!"

As I later learned, stories such as that were recycled from German TV and we couldn't necessarily run off to Malta, but I was very impressed.

Although I had visited Europe several times, I never gave much thought to returning other than a vague desire to revisit the Greek island of Mykonos.

After Prof. Stehr informed me I'd been hired, he arranged for me to attend *Europa Kolleg* and I sent off a money order to pay for it. The grand total for tuition, room and board for the four-week course came to just under $600.

Once in Kassel, I occasionally wondered if I really had the job. Not only did it seem too good to be true, but I had never had any personal contact with anyone in Cologne. Before leaving the U.S., I received a letter from Werner Hadulla of Transtel telling me what my salary would be and how much money the government would deduct for taxes, etc. I wrote to him from Kassel asking where I should go when I got to Cologne. There was no immediate response, so I went to the *Postamt* (post office) and phoned. I was transferred to another man who gave me the name of a hotel. It was a relief to know it wasn't a hoax and they hadn't forgotten me.

Before cell phones and prepaid phone cards, the post office was the place to go for anyone who was phoneless. A clerk would assign you to a certain booth or *Kabine*. After you made the call, the clerk would tell you how much you owed. No fumbling with coins.

A lift to Cologne

When school ended, one of the French guys offered me a ride to Cologne, which I gladly accepted. He had a Renault 4, a boxy bottom-of-the-line little car that had the gearshift lever sticking out of the dashboard. The trip was awkward because he didn't speak English, I knew hardly any French and neither of us could converse in German even though we had just finished the course.

After a drive of about two hours, he dropped me off at the hotel, located on a noisy intersection where several bus and *Strassenbahn* lines converged. It was an older building. The rooms were above a row of shops, reached by climbing a narrow wooden stairway.

Once inside, I studied a map and figured out where the *Deutsche Welle* was. I walked there, a couple of kilometers south along a major street, so I'd know where to go in the morning. It was easy to spot – a modern 34-story skyscraper towering over other buildings only a few stories high. I was glad to know I'd be working on the southern edge of the city and wouldn't have to commute downtown.

With a population of nearly one million, Cologne – called Köln by the Germans – was one of the biggest cities in Germany. In fact, it was THE biggest city during the Middle Ages. Almost all of Cologne was flattened during World War Two. There are photos showing little more than the famous Gothic cathedral standing amid the ruins along the Rhine.

Like millions of other people, I had jumped off the train in Cologne on my first visit to Europe years before just to look at the cathedral, never dreaming I'd wind up living there.

Compared with more sophisticated cities such as Munich, Cologne had a wild and gritty feeling. The biggest annual event is *Karneval,* which is equivalent to Carnival in Rio or Mardi Gras in New Orleans. It's a time for costumes and parades, when it's almost legal to be drunk and disorderly. On one of the *Karneval* days, women armed with scissors roam around snipping neckties off unsuspecting men.

On my first full day, I walked to work and met everyone including two other reporters who were hired along with me. They had started a few weeks earlier because my arrival was delayed by the language course.

One of my new colleagues was Mary Beth Lamb, a perky, attractive blonde in her 20s. She was a recent Phi Beta Kappa graduate of the University of Wisconsin who had worked as an intern at the PBS station in Madison. Despite her lack of experience in TV news, she caught on quickly and did a professional job right from the start. Mary Beth spoke German fluently, having attended a university in the southwestern city of Freiburg for one year. Among her talents was playing woodwinds in the University of Wisconsin Symphony Orchestra.

The other reporter was Peter Morello, a stocky guy with Sicilian roots who always looked as if he needed a shave. He and his wife, a Danish blonde named Lone (LOW-nah), had arrived from Grand Junction, Colorado, where he had worked as a TV reporter. Lone, who was multilingual, taught German at a high school there. Peter met her in Copenhagen while working as a room service waiter at a high class hotel. He listed reggae icon Bob Marley among the biggest celebrities he had served. Peter claimed his German was good and he spoke Danish like a native.

Fast Forward: months later I was attending a small gathering at Peter's place. While he was in the kitchen, Lone remarked, "You know, it's tough when we have visitors from Denmark and we're watching TV. I have to tell them what's happening in Danish, then explain it to Peter in English." So much for his linguistic abilities.

Peter had a remarkable knowledge of politics – not only German or American, but politics anywhere in the world. One of his special talents was his ability to whistle or hum the theme song from any American TV show. He also got a few laughs by walking around singing, *Don't Cry for Me, Deutsche Welle,* to the melody of the popular song from *Evita.*

Peter turned out to be one of the world's greatest gossips. He enjoyed prying information out of people, especially personal tidbits, then broadcasting it all over the building. One of our German colleagues, a woman, once described him as "the walking *Bild Zeitung,"* a reference to the national tabloid newspaper.

One Monday morning Peter was quizzing me relentlessly about what I had done during the weekend. I was being as tight-lipped as possible, so he blurted out, "You know something? Your private life is too private."

I mentioned that later to Mary Beth and she said, "Yeah. He told me the same thing."

Peter, Mary Beth and I each started at a salary of 6,000 DM (Deutsch marks) per month. That was roughly $2,270, but the dollar amount didn't mean much because the exchange rate fluctuated constantly. Peter claimed our German colleagues were on the brink of rioting when they learned how lavishly we were being paid. Although Peter had doubled his previous salary, Mary Beth undoubtedly was earning considerably more and I was earning less, the equal pay didn't bother me. I was thrilled to have what looked like a fantastic job regardless of the pay.

Introducing Rex and Rendy

European Journal had been on the air for several years before we came aboard, but it was frightfully out of step by U.S. standards despite the fact that a few Americans worked on the show as freelancers. Noticeably absent from the reporters' packages were standups and signoffs.

Whenever TV news professionals in the U.S. were asked to critique the show, they always agreed it looked about

20 years behind the times. "Sixties," they said.

We presumably had been brought in to Americanize and energize the show.

The anchor/producer was Rex Ellis, an Englishman who had been knocking around the news business for many years in various parts of the world. Rex was a large guy who vaguely resembled the late Libyan dictator Moammar Gadhafi except that Rex's unruly black hair was a bit thin on top. He spoke his own brand of German, fluent but mangled. I always thought if there were an organization such as the Society for the Protection of the German Language, Rex would have had a bounty on his head.

The boss was Wolfgang Rendelsmann. He was constantly on a diet and his weight varied dramatically, but he never quite got down to normal size. His rumpled clothes and tousled brown hair gave him the look of an absent-minded professor when he peered over his clear plastic-framed glasses. As executive producer of the show, he approved all story ideas and had the final say on everything except when overruled by the officials in Bonn.

Rendelsmann spoke English with barely an accent but had problems with grammar. He would say things such as, "What do you mean?" instead of, "What do you think?" But we all understood. As with any German in authority, he was always addressed as Herr Rendelsmann. Staffers often referred to him as Rendy, but only Rex called him Rendy to his face. Rex even addressed him as Wolfgang once in a while. After we got to know him, we nicknamed him *die Qualle* – jellyfish – because he always seemed to have trouble making decisions.

The *European Journal* offices were spread out between the fifth and eighth floors, apparently because the expansion of the staff was a new development and a block of adjoining rooms had not been available. Since it was a modern building, occupied for only three years, the offices had plate glass windows that couldn't be opened, covered with vertical blinds.

Peter, Mary Beth and I shared an office on one floor.

Rex and Rendelsmann were on two other floors. That was fine because Rex's office was often chaotic and we needed quiet to work on our scripts and use the phone to set up stories. The three of us would bounce ideas off each other and proofread each other's scripts. Whenever Peter wanted our opinion, he preferred to stand and do a dramatic reading rather than simply hand over his copy.

About 1,300 people worked at the *Deutsche Welle*. You could get an idea of how international the operation was by having a meal in the huge ground floor cafeteria that served a choice of three reasonably priced full-course lunches each day. Most of the employees were German of course, but there was also a sprinkling of Asians, Africans and South Americans, not to mention North Americans, Brits, Australians and East Europeans.

Although the cafeteria was open only for lunch, there was a separate snack bar where one could buy coffee, sandwiches, sweet rolls and cake as well as alcohol. The bar opened every morning promptly at 10, and there were always a few employees bellying up shortly thereafter to jumpstart their day with a beer or a shot of cognac.

People who didn't have time to eat before they left home could grab a standard high fat breakfast sandwich of cheese or salami inside a heavily buttered *Brotchen*.

The coffee was so bad I started putting cream in it for the first time in my life. I eventually got in the habit of bringing a jar of Nescafé instant to the office and mixing it with boiling water intended for tea.

The Germans called the cafeteria the *Kantine*, pronounced cantina. The snack bar was known as the C*afeteria*. A little confusing for English-speakers.

Another language oddity: while Americans use the word gymnasium to describe a hall devoted to exercise or athletic activities, *Gymnasium* is the German word for the entire school, specifically high school. The German word for gymnasium is *Sporthalle*. *Alles klar?*

New meaning to the word elegant

The most urgent thing I had to do was find a place to live. Peter recommended I see a man in the personnel department named Herr Grull whose job it was to help new employees get settled. The first thing he did was apply for residence permits for us. We gave him our passports and he took care of it.

He had helped Peter find a fantastic apartment. Just before Peter walked into Grull's office, a man who lived nearby had phoned. He owned a three-story section of a row house that included two apartments. He lived on the ground floor. His son had just vacated the apartment above and he wanted to rent it out.

Peter and Grull went to look at it and Peter couldn't believe how nice it was. The apartment was completely furnished. The main floor consisted of a huge living room, an eat-in kitchen and a bathroom. Crammed into the second level, beneath a sloping roof, were two bedrooms. The man had never rented the place before and didn't know how much to charge. He asked Peter if 600 DM ($230) would be all right. Peter gasped because the price was so low and quickly pressed a fistful of marks into his hands.

I caught up with Herr Grull in his office. He spoke excellent English with a British accent, dressed in tweeds and had a ruddy complexion, piercing blue eyes with a distant look and brown hair combed straight back. He happened to have a new listing for a nearby apartment described as "elegant."

We made an appointment to see it and met the landlord there, a tall older man with a full head of white hair. The apartment, on the ground floor of a newer building, was not exactly what I would call elegant. It was essentially one large room stretching from an interior door to floor-to-ceiling plate glass windows which opened onto a fenced patio. Off on one side were three doorways leading to the bathroom, kitchen and bedroom.

The bedroom was very odd, more of a compartment than a room. It had a doorway but no door and was just big enough to accommodate a large mattress, nothing more, with about one foot of space on each side.

The bathroom had all the fixtures, but I was surprised to see there was nothing in the kitchen, absolutely nothing but capped pipes sticking out of the wall – no cabinets, no appliances, not even a sink. Grull explained that such a thing was normal because Germans like to take their cabinets and sinks with them when they move. He said finding an apartment that included those things was nearly impossible.

When I told him I had serious reservations about the place, he stood in the middle of the room, spread his arms wide, tilted his head back and said he had never seen such a fantastic apartment.

Although the thought of buying a kitchen sink and cabinets in addition to furniture horrified me, the *Deutsche Welle* was only paying for my hotel for a week and I had to live somewhere, so I reluctantly signed the lease and moved in.

Fast forward: Herr Grull was visiting our office months later. When he started to leave, he walked into the coat closet and thrashed around as we yelled, "Left, left. The door is on the left." After he was gone, I asked, "What the hell was that?" Mary Beth said, "Oh, didn't you know? He's legally blind." And he was the guy who told me how great the apartment looked.

My next task was to find a real apartment as soon as possible. I suspected there must be better-equipped places. I told Mary Beth what had happened. She volunteered to help me the following weekend.

During the week, I was in the office for less than an hour one morning when Rex handed me a telegram from my father saying Mr. Sluggo would be arriving at the airport. In 30 minutes.

Rex thought Mr. Sluggo was a person until I explained he was my dog.

A Temporary European

I know Mr. Sluggo was a goofy name, but that's the best I could come up with when he was a puppy. It hardly fit a dog as cute as he was. Despite being a Sheltie and coming from a mall pet shop, he never barked and was born well-trained. I never used a leash. He would always stay next to me when we walked and sat down automatically when we got to a curb.

Sluggo's arrival was a big surprise. I hadn't said a thing to my father about shipping him because I wanted to get an apartment first. He apparently thought since I was scheduled to be in Cologne, it was OK. Before I had time to panic, Rex arranged for a large truck to meet me at the back door and take me to the airport.

Although the Turkish driver spoke no English, we somehow managed to communicate. We reached the airport moments after the dog arrived along with my steamer trunk. I was eager to get him out of the box as soon as possible because he'd been traveling for 18 hours.

Doing the paperwork seemed to take forever but it actually went smoothly. Once we were outside, the driver commented that my dog didn't seem to know me. He did, but judging from the way he was staggering around, he apparently had been drugged for the flight. The driver insisted the dog ride up front with us. I hesitated because his underside was soaked with urine, but I popped open the trunk, found a towel and placed it under him.

By the time we got to the apartment about 20 minutes later, Mr. Sluggo had recovered. He was jumping around and the driver was happy.

So there I was, sitting on the floor of the empty apartment in a strange country with a few possessions and my dog, wondering how I was going to find a real place to live.

At last, an apartment

Apartments were relatively scarce in Cologne. The best way to find one was to check the ads in the Saturday newspaper. People who were eager to get a head start on their search would go downtown Friday night and buy the first edition from newsboys hawking them on the street outside theaters and cafés.

I bought a paper early Saturday and met Mary Beth at her sparsely furnished apartment. She did the translating as we looked over the ads, picking half a dozen places to check out. Since Mary Beth didn't have a phone yet, we went to a nearby phone booth with a pocketful of coins. She made appointments, then I made the rounds.

After looking at several apartments, I found one I liked. The landlord, Helmut Brühl, spoke enough English so we could converse. He was 30-something, tall and thin. He wore glasses, had dark hair and a full mustache.

The apartment was in the basement of a three-story house. It had its own entrance on the side of the house, down a short staircase beyond the entrance to the upper floors. Inside the outer door, half a step down on the right, was a closet-sized room containing a toilet. Down a few steps to the left with a right turn at the bottom was an inner door that opened into the kitchen. Diagonally across on the right, along the outside wall, was the bathroom, which featured a shower and wash basin. On the left was a short hallway that led to a large room furnished with a bed, a desk and a table. The makeshift bed was two twin mattresses laid side-by-side on thick sheets of plywood supported by cinder blocks.

The apartment was in the back of the building, partly underground, with the windows looking out on the yard a few inches above the grass. It had typical German windows that can be cracked open a few inches at the top or opened all the way from one side, depending on which way the handle is turned.

There were no screens. In fact, I don't ever recall

A Temporary European

seeing a window screen anywhere in Europe. I never saw a mosquito either. That explains the lack of screens.

Outside the windows were *Rolläden*, heavy metal blinds that are rolled up inside the wall and can be lowered at night.

German houses and apartments generally don't have closets. Instead, the people use what's known as a *Schrank* or cabinet. They're similar to what Americans call an armoire. They have double doors which are often covered with full-length mirrors. They usually have rods inside on which to hang clothing, plus some shelves.

There were curtained alcoves on either side of the windows in the main room. One contained a *Schrank* and the other side had clothing rods, providing more storage space than most apartments.

There were no cabinets in the kitchen, just a sink, a refrigerator, a small table and a large empty space below the window. Herr Brühl promised to go to IKEA, the Swedish home furnishings store, and buy cabinets to fill the void. He did so a few days later, getting several units that sat below the window and supported a counter about six feet long.

I had never heard of IKEA (pronounced ee-KAY-uh in Germany) until I moved to Europe because the first one didn't open in the United States until 1985. But after I'd been to one, I became a big fan. I quickly became a convert to the German custom of using down comforters instead of blankets. In fact, I haven't used a blanket since. IKEA sold bedding at very reasonable prices compared with the big department stores.

In addition to buying cabinets, Brühl had wall-to-wall carpeting installed in the hallway and living room.

The refrigerator was typical of what's found in many German apartments, something we might call a Ken & Barbie model. They're less than half as large as what we're used to in the United States and made to fit under a counter like a dishwasher. There's no freezer except for a slot at the top designed for ice trays. It's just big enough to slip in a hamburger or anything else that's less than two inches thick.

Apartments in Germany were usually rented "warm," meaning utilities were included. My rent was 480 DM plus 60 DM for *Nebenkosten* for a total of 540 DM ($208). *Neben* means alongside or next to. *Kosten* means costs. The word refers to such things as water, heat, electricity, garbage pickup and yard care.

Getting used to marks instead of dollars was a gradual process. If I had converted all prices to dollars, I might not have bought anything because the prices would have seemed too high – except for the reasonable rent. After a few months, I became accustomed to what everything cost in marks and rarely thought in dollars.

The *Strassenbahn* ran right past the apartment, but it didn't bother me although I could hear it and even feel it rumble by during the quiet early morning hours. Looking on the bright side, the nearest stop *(Haltestelle)* was only half a block away.

One good thing about the apartment was its convenient location just one kilometer (5/8 of a mile) from the office. That allowed me to walk to work and even get home around noon for a quick outing with the dog.

My place was roughly halfway between the *Deutsche Welle* and the bank of the Rhine, where Sluggo and I often joined the locals for a Sunday afternoon stroll.

It was a pleasant walk to either the river or the office. Half a block south of the apartment was a wide tree-lined boulevard with a path down the middle that ran from the Rhine to the *Deutsche Welle* and far beyond. Long ago, it marked the outer limits of the city.

After I signed the lease, I met with Herr Grull and the other landlord to cancel the lease on the elegant apartment. Fortunately I escaped any penalty. I only had to pay for the few days I had stayed in the place.

At the new apartment, Herr Brühl informed me it was the custom in Germany for tenants to paint the walls on either their arrival or departure. I chose to do it immediately, buying a large plastic tub of white paint from a home improvement chain called Bauhaus and hauling it back on the *Strassenbahn*. The same *Strassenbahn* that passed the apartment stopped in front of Bauhaus, eight stops away, so I didn't have to lug the paint far.

Since Germans didn't have checkbooks as we know them, I followed local custom and arranged for my bank to automatically transfer my rent payment to Herr Brühl's bank each month. That was the only monthly bill I had except for the phone. I paid that by filling out a money transfer form and dropping it off at my bank.

Brühl apparently had bought the building only recently. When I moved in, the back yard was a jungle. But within a few months, he had it looking great.

He later added a block of cabinets to my room that he no longer needed. Typically, cabinets designed for the living room come in modular units that can be arranged in any way. Usually three very low one-drawer chests are placed side-by-side along the wall forming the base. Topping them will be a china cabinet with glass doors sandwiched between other cabinets with wooden doors.

The cabinets almost filled the wall opposite the windows, making the apartment much more livable. They had more drawers and shelves than I could possibly use.

Shooting the *Deutsche Welle* way

Once I moved into the real apartment, I could concentrate on my work. The first thing I had to do was come up with story ideas. After several days at the typewriter, I submitted 40 suggestions to Rendelsmann.

He rejected all of them, saying the blanket rejection was to show me I didn't "know Europe." But I eventually lobbied him into approving a few.

The first story I did was about the school for craftsmen

attended by my three former French classmates. The story turned out well but it took longer to shoot than expected because I didn't have the logistics and timing down, primarily how long it took to drive from one place to another. In addition to shooting at the school, which was northwest of Cologne, we had to go to a church north of the city and a castle to the south to film the men working.

The shoot wound up taking two days instead of one. But it was a valuable lesson. I gradually learned to build more padding into my shooting schedules. Before long, I could block out a plan to shoot stories in different locations over several days.

For a quick shoot within a couple of hours from Cologne, we generally used a staff camera crew, called a *Hausteam,* which consisted of a photographer, a sound man or woman and an assistant who took care of the lights and did a lot of schlepping. If a reporter had to go to Paris for only one story, the *DW* would hire a local freelance crew and the reporter would travel there by plane or train. But if there were several stories, a *Hausteam* would be used and we would travel by company car. It was all based on the most cost effective way of getting the stories done.

One of my early stories was a piece about an old salt mine near Braunschweig where the government was experimenting with the storage of nuclear waste.

Since it was in Germany just a few hours north of Cologne, I traveled with a *Hausteam* headed by an Iranian cameraman known only as Yazdi. We got there late in the afternoon, stayed in a hotel overnight and reported to the mine early the next morning.

Just doing that story illustrated the greatest aspect of the job – learning. If I hadn't done that piece, I never would have known what it was like to travel 2,500 feet underground in a huge, clanking elevator and feel the temperature climb as I descended into the Earth.

Dealing with Yazdi could be a problem. Although he

A Temporary European

was a nice guy and an enthusiastic photographer, he liked a lot of camera movement. As I was memorizing my lines for the standup inside the mine, Yazdi yelled that he was ready. I looked over and noticed he had the camera pointed at the ceiling. Since I was new and didn't want to rock the boat, I didn't protest. I tried to pad out the beginning of my statement so I could discard it in the editing room and start with the camera already on me, but I couldn't think fast enough. As it turned out, the camera panned along the ceiling and reached me seconds before I finished talking. Just what Yazdi wanted.

Shooting the ceiling wasn't unusual in Europe. Whenever there was a story about a conference on a European newscast, there was a good chance it would open with a pan down from a chandelier. Morello joked that there was so much camera movement on Italian TV that it looked as if the photographers shot entire stories without ever turning off the camera.

I had a tussle on the salt mine story with Rex, who seemed to consider himself an expert on everything. After I handed in my script, he changed the name Braunschweig to Brunswick because that's what the British called it. Rex assumed the entire English-speaking world followed suit. In order to settle the argument, I brought in a *National Geographic* map and explained to Rex and Rendelsmann that the *Geographic* was the number one U.S. authority on place names and it used Braunschweig. It worked.

Rex wasn't quite as knowledgeable about American English as he thought. After I wrote a story about declining car sales in Europe, Rex called and alerted me that he was going to change the word "car" to "auto" because, he said, "that's what Americans call their cars." I told him only people who sell cars or insure them call them "autos." The drivers say "car." He believed me and didn't change it.

Once Rex used the word "scheme" in a script. I pointed out that although scheme may be a perfectly good synonym for "plan" in Britain, it often has a negative connotation in the USA.

Another word with different meanings that popped up was "tabled." Rex wrote that something had been tabled at a meeting. In Britain, tabled means to put it on the agenda, which is what happened in his story, whereas in the United States it means to set it aside.

One of my first "foreign" assignments took me to Vienna for a rather dry story on an East-West organization called the International Institute for Applied Systems Analysis.

Since it was more efficient to knock out two stories, Rendelsmann asked me to shoot some MOS (Man on the Street) interviews and a standup to flesh out a *Dup* (a copy of a piece from German TV) about the famous coffee houses of Vienna. There were well over 150 of them. Each had its own character. For example, the Café Central, where Trotsky planned the Russian revolution, was known for its huge columns. The Café Mozart was said to be a favorite of Soviet KGB agents during the Cold War.

Legend has it that the Viennese first became aware of coffee in the late 1600s when Turkish invaders departed, leaving bags of coffee beans behind. They did a taste test, then developed coffee brewing into an art.

Working with a local freelance crew, I interviewed customers at a café called the Schwarzenberg. Their responses echoed the results of surveys that said people visited coffee houses primarily to socialize. Drinking coffee was secondary. Sampling the heavenly pastries came in farther down the list. One of the better-known local delicacies was the *Sachertorte*, which might be described as a belt-busting overdose of chocolate.

About 80 percent of the patrons were regulars. Some showed up every day. One great thing about the coffee houses was that the waiters never tried to hustle anyone for a refill. A customer could buy one cup and nurse it all day. Every coffee house provided a wide selection of newspapers for those who wanted to lounge around. Some patrons read books. Others scribbled intently in journals, looking as if they were writing books.

People at every table seemed to be wrapped up in their own business. When we set up the camera and lights to shoot my standup as I sat at one of the tables, no one seemed to pay the least bit of attention.

While talking with one man in the café prior to an interview, I was speaking English but throwing in a few German words, showing off my newfound language skills. Almost scolding, he said, "Don't mix English and German. It's too confusing. Speak one or the other." At first I was taken aback, but I realized what he said made sense. After that, I was always careful never to mix languages unless it was unavoidable.

I and other Americans routinely used certain German words when we spoke among ourselves. We'd say *Bahnhof* and *Strassenbahn*, never train station or streetcar. One colleague suggested that we adopted certain German names because we never used the English equivalent at home. Streetcar would be a good example. On the other hand, since airport was a word we used all the time, we continued using it rather than saying *Flughaven.*

Not all English expressions can be translated directly into German and vice versa. Peter had first-hand experience with that when he interviewed the late Franz Josef Strauss, the rotund, owl-faced prime minister of Bavaria. When Peter asked a question, Strauss replied in English, "That's self-understandable."

Of course there's no such expression in English. You'd have to say, "That's obvious," or "That's self-evident." But Strauss was simply doing a direct translation of the common German word, *"Selbstverständlich."*

I discovered another example of an unsuitable translation while eating dinner with a German co-worker and her parents at their home.

Although I was quite satisfied with the meal, they kept encouraging me to eat more. I said, *"Nein, danke. Ich bin voll,"* a literal translation of, "No thanks. I'm full."

Almost in unison, the three of them advised, "Don't say that. It means you're drunk."

I later learned the correct phrase is, *"Ich bin satt."* Satt means full, satisfied or satiated.

On another of my early trips to Vienna, I inadvertently violated one of Rex's taboos regarding language. I was doing a story about a political crisis in Austria. The best person to interview was the leader of the Socialist faction in Parliament. He didn't speak English, so we filmed him answering my questions in German.

Back in Cologne, Rex almost had a stroke. I hadn't realized it but he had established an unwritten rule that interviews could be done only in English, no matter how incomprehensible it might be. I was told Rex had even thrown out sound bites that weren't in English.

That struck me as stupid. I wasn't the only one. I appealed to Rendslemann and wound up getting permission to do the piece showing the man speaking German while someone voiced an English translation.

After that, interviews in any language were fair game.

The photographers were still shooting film when Mary Beth, Peter and I started, although U.S. TV stations had switched to videotape some years earlier.

There was a film processing lab in the back of the building. Whenever it was closed, camera crews left the film in a large wooden box outside the door.

One of the *DW* legends was the story of a camera crew that returned on the weekend from a long shoot in Africa. The film was deposited in the box, but when the photographer went to check on it Monday, the folks in the lab said they'd never seen it. Everyone surmised that the Turkish cleaning crew had mistakenly thrown it away. Soon after that, a sign was placed over the box that said in Turkish, "This is not trash." There must be some truth to the story because I saw the sign myself.

The *Deutsche Welle* style of shooting and editing was strange compared with the USA. The photographer shot silent film and the sound man lugged around a huge contraption that recorded the audio on a separate reel. As in Hollywood, the assistant would either use a clapperboard or clap his hands in front of the lens as each scene began.

That would aid the editor in synchronizing the sound and picture, lining up the two strips of film so the clap was heard at exactly the same instant the hands or clapper came together. It worked in principle, but often during the editing the sound would go out of sync and have to be adjusted. I had the feeling they sometimes stretched the film to make it work.

All the staff film editors were women. German slang for editor is *Cutter*. A woman editor is known as a *Cutterin*, with the suffix *-in* denoting a female.

We quickly learned German film slang, which was useful because some of the editors as well as some freelance photographers didn't speak much English. For example, natural sound was known as *Atmo*, a sound bite was an *O-Ton* and a closeup was a *Grossaufnahme*.

When we started, the *Deutsche Welle* style of editing was truly bizarre. The editor would cut the pictures first with no input from the reporter, assembling them however she saw fit. Then the reporters were supposed to watch the finished piece, take notes and write their script to fit the pictures.

That sounded like a nightmare to us, so Peter, Mary Beth and I immediately started pressing for the American system, which was to record the voice track first, then cut the pictures. Meanwhile, we cheated by writing our scripts in advance as usual. Of course we always watched our films and made a shot list before writing anything in order to make sure the words and pictures would work together. The worst thing that could happen was having more script than pictures.

Once in the editing room, we'd tell the editor which pictures and sound bites we wanted and how long each scene should run. But the recording of the voice track still came last, and that was always tricky.

Each Thursday we'd gather in a studio for a *Sprachaufnahme* (voice recording session). An engineer would operate a huge control board as each reporter took turns sitting in an adjoining soundproof room where our film was projected onto a huge screen.

It was a typical studio where the engineer could see us through a large window. We would try to read our script in sync with the picture, glancing between the text and the screen. But it never worked the same as it had in the editing room. Sometimes we had to add pauses. Other times we had to cut a few words or read as fast as we could in order to make everything fit. It was nerve-wracking and the often erratic pacing on the finished piece sounded weird.

The Americanization of *EJ*

Peter, Mary Beth and I decided we had to drag the *Deutsche Welle* into the 20th Century, so we got together several times to discuss how to improve the show. We came up with five typed pages of recommendations which I put into final form.

At the top of the list was recording the voice track first. The editors fought us, arguing they would be deprived of their artistic expression. Somehow we got the point across that we were doing news, not art. Of course there's no question that an editor needs an artistic sense, but ideally the finished piece should be a marriage of both the pictures and narration.

Eventually we won. The moaning and groaning stopped. We started doing the *Sprachaufnahme* first, then walked into the editing room with our voice track in hand.

Another thing the editors had to adjust to was our use

of shorter scenes. They complained our scenes were so short they got whiplash. The German practice was to use much longer scenes with not much attention paid to what we considered to be unnecessary camera movement.

Fortunately the *Deutsche Welle* started using videotape less than a year after we arrived. The photographers grumbled for a while, arguing that film had a better look, but they soon got used to the change.

One advantage to shooting video was that the sound was recorded directly onto the tape, meaning there was no worry about synchronization.

Since bulky recorders were not required for video cameras, freelance crews started using only two people. But the *Deutsche Welle* stuck with three.

Back when newsrooms in the U.S. used film, the sound was recorded magnetically along the edge of the film. There was no second reel just for sound.

At first, there was a misunderstanding over standups and signoffs. Some Germans indicated they thought we wanted to be on camera just so we could get our faces on TV. We explained that the standups were intended to add variety to a story as well as demonstrate that the reporter was actually at the scene.

I never liked doing standups. First of all, they're tough to write, especially if they'll be in the middle of the piece. They can be very useful as bridges, providing you can lay out the story in your head in advance. Producing a story is like putting a jigsaw puzzle together backwards. You try to gather all the pieces without knowing what the final picture will look like, thinking ahead to what you'll need in the editing room. It's very challenging, but that may be one reason it's so much fun.

I tried to avoid doing standups wherever I might attract an audience, finding a spot where there was activity behind me but no one nearby.

We all did at least one standup in front of the Brandenburg Gate before the Berlin Wall fell. One freelancer told me tourists broke into applause when he finished. That would have made me melt in embarrassment.

On the other hand, doing a standup in the middle of a big crowd is no problem because no one pays any attention. I once did a standup on a platform in the Cologne *Hauptbahnhof* (main train station), walking toward the photographer as he moved backward. One take ended when he bumped into someone. The man complained excitedly, in German of course, "You're not supposed to walk backwards in the train station!"

One word in our critique that made Rendelsmann wince and presumably sent Rex into orbit was "boring." We criticized the format of the program, saying it had the rhythm of a punch press. We called for more variety in the pacing, pointing out that the audience knew there would always be eight stories, each running approximately two and a half minutes with each lead-in averaging 25 seconds. The opening of the show, which was animation, was so long and slow that much of the audience might doze off before the first story came up. We recommended tightening it and getting different theme music.

A friend in Phoenix watched the show after I mentioned I was working on it. He said the theme music was the same as a porno film called *Sex World*. Apparently both *European Journal* and the porno producers bought the same music as part of a package of theme songs.

We suggested other things that were common in the United States but unknown in Cologne such as anchors anchoring from the field, putting a reporter on the set to intro his or her package and doing interviews on the set.

We stressed relevance, saying some stories were of little or no interest to U.S. viewers. And we suggested minimal use of the aforementioned *Dups* and trade show films. *Dup* is an abbreviation for the German word *Duplikat.* The difference in visual quality between one of our stories and a *Dup* was sometimes so radical that it looked like the pieces came from two different programs, which they did.

Although *European Journal* was broadcast on many PBS stations, most were what might be described as second tier stations. That is, in bigger cities where there were two PBS channels, one would broadcast the best offerings and the other would run the leftovers. Management said the better stations "didn't have room in their schedules for *European Journal.*" We insisted they could always make room for a program they liked.

Eventually most of our suggestions were adopted and it brightened up the show.

As backward as it was, *European Journal* had made considerable progress since its beginning a few years earlier. One day Peter walked in with a tape he said was the very first show. It was incredible. The anchors, Stephen Belless and Kathleen Lawton, sat side-by-side behind a desk with their hands practically glued to the desk, staring straight into the camera. The only body part that seemed to move was their lips. They barely acknowledged the presence of each other. When Belless did move his head, you could see his pony tail flip around. It was no wonder they had trouble getting stations to broadcast the program.

When we arrived, Belless was one of the directors. He was very intense, not what you'd call one of the guys, so he wasn't someone you wanted to argue with. I wasn't familiar with his background, but it was clear he didn't know much about television news. He was always experimenting with things like the fonts – the names and titles of people seen at the bottom of the screen.

A font, short for vidifont, is also known in some areas as a super, short for superimposition, or CG, meaning character generator. Belless might slide the fonts in from the side, which was distracting, instead of simply popping them in, as was the usual custom. It looked as if he was trying to re-invent TV news.

The Germans have a great word for fonts – *Bauchbinder,* **which means belly binder.**
Speaking of literal words, one of my favorites is *Staubsauger* **– the German word for vacuum cleaner. It translates into English as dust sucker.**

Kathleen Lawton was co-anchoring with Rex when we arrived. She came from Los Angeles, had a pale complexion and long black hair that fell to her shoulders. She always dressed in black and spoke in a deep throaty voice. It was no surprise that some people referred to her as Vampira. She and Rex together were very laid back, almost funereal in their delivery.

Kathleen told me she was once recognized in a supermarket in Santa Monica. One thing I liked about *European Journal* was that I wouldn't be recognized because I lived across the ocean from the viewers.

After a few months, Kathleen began making occasional trips to the States and Mary Beth became the co-anchor. She was lively and tried to relate to Rex, but he more or less ignored her.

Mary Beth jokingly referred to Rex as "sexy Rexy." Not to his face, of course.

The show was taped on Friday afternoon, then shipped on Lufthansa to Dr. Stehr. He in turn fed it to subscribers via satellite at Oregon Public Broadcasting.

The professor always had what was called a *Reserve-rolle* standing by in Oregon in case the tape got misplaced along the way. That was a special undated and dull version of the show consisting of rerun stories as well as *Dups.*

It often took hours to finish taping because the director would stop and re-record every time something went wrong. That could include anything from an anchor stumbling over a word to the wrong graphic or font coming up. I couldn't help wondering what would happen if they ever put a show on the air live.

Years later, I found out. They had booked half an hour of satellite time for a live broadcast, but started 10 minutes late, resulting in the last 10 minutes of the show being cut off.

Belless had a German girlfriend named Cornelia Baumsteiger. Her last name in English means tree climber. She worked as a production assistant and it seemed as if her main job was to misspell the fonts. She was kind of snooty, always wore a strange orange makeup and seemed to glide around. That earned her the nickname *die Schlange,* or the snake.

When I first got there, Cornelia asked me if I spoke German. I said, "Only in self-defense." – stealing a line Johnny Carson used when asked if he spoke French. I don't think she got it.

With eccentrics like Ellis and Belless around, I started wondering if being weird was a prerequisite for being an expatriate. Was I already weird and didn't know it, or would I become weird if I stayed too long?

Storing the dog

Since I had to travel often, finding temporary accommodation for Mr. Sluggo was a top priority. It wasn't easy because vets in Germany didn't board pets as they did in the United States. That may have something to do with the fact that many of them had their offices in regular houses or apartment buildings where there obviously would be problems with noise during the night.

The first time I had to be away, a Transtel secretary arranged for the dog to stay with an elderly woman she knew. I didn't care for that arrangement because the woman lived in a huge block-long apartment building on a busy street. Not the best situation for dog walks. She never left the apartment anyway, so the secretary dropped by to take him out.

Luckily, one of my German colleagues, Ulla Wissemann, told me her parents would be glad to care for him. They were retired and lived in a row house in a new housing development south of Bonn, a 30 minute drive from my apartment, mostly on the autobahn.

That turned out to be ideal. The Wissemanns enjoyed having Sluggo and he got along fine with their poodle, Yo-yo (spelled Jo-jo in German). He was so-named because he bounced up and down like a you-know-what.

All I had to do was make sure I didn't abuse the dog-sitting privilege by overusing it.

Visiting with the Wissemanns was a good opportunity to improve my German. When I picked up Sluggo, they would insist I drink a glass of sherry. I usually stayed for at least half an hour, discussing any number of things. A typical conversation would have Herr Wissemann, a retired Air Force pilot, railing against big trucks on the autobahn. He thought they should all be put on trains so there would be more room for cars.

The Wissemanns were the automatic first choice for dog-sitters. Twice, when I had to be away for a full week, I had to find an alternative. One was a kennel located halfway to Aachen, a 45 minute drive from my apartment. The other was way out in the country east of Cologne, a house with a huge fenced yard where a dozen boarded dogs ran around in a pack. I was worried about Sluggo being bitten, but he survived unscathed.

On rare occasions when the Wissemanns couldn't do it, Rendelsmann took Mr. Sluggo. He had volunteered to keep him whenever I got in a bind. Since he was my boss, I never would have thought of asking him.

Once after caring for Sluggo, Rendelsmann brought him to the office to save me the trip to his home in the suburbs. He got in before I did and started looking through material on his desk. After a few moments, he noticed Sluggo had disappeared. Racing down the hall, he found him waiting for an elevator and coaxed him back to the office. It was a precarious situation. With eight elevators serving 34 floors, if Sluggo had entered one, it might have been years before he was found.

Rendelsmann and I developed what I believed was a cordial relationship. I always tried to handle him delicately because he would lose his temper whenever something went wrong, no matter how trivial. When I walked into his office, he might be pounding his desk because he just had an argument on the phone with Rex. Or he might be grumbling because Mary Beth rounded off her overtime to the nearest 15 minutes instead of an hour. I never wanted to be one of those who triggered a tantrum.

After I'd been there for a while, Rendelsmann would introduce me as his "best reporter," something I found embarrassing. To paraphrase an old Hollywood expression, I thought I was only as good as my last story.

Buying wheels

Getting Mr. Sluggo to the dog-sitters was the main reason I needed my own transportation. Reaching the Wissemann house on public transit would have required an intercity train ride plus at least one local bus, with the whole trip taking at least an hour, not counting waiting.

I also needed a car to get to the laundromat. I was tired of traveling there on the *Strassenbahn*, lugging huge plastic bags. I went early Sunday morning to avoid the crowds and it was always an adventure. One morning, a truck driver with a big rig parked outside was sitting on a bench watching the dryers, clad only in his shorts. He obviously wanted to clean as many clothes as possible.

I never considered buying a washer and dryer because they were smaller than the U.S. models and cost a lot more.

With a low resale value, it didn't seem practical for a two-year stay.

I couldn't afford to buy anything when I first arrived in Cologne anyway because I was still paying the mortgage on my house in Ohio – $863 a month – and it took eight months to sell. I was so broke my father had to loan me money for the final payment.

I also wanted transportation for shopping, weekend getaways and vacations.

Less than a year after arriving, having saved some money, I made the rounds of half a dozen car dealers. I didn't see anything I liked until I got to the Renault dealer. Behind the new cars in a big warehouse-sized showroom were dozens of used cars. Poking above the vehicles along the back wall was a metallic brown Renault 4 panel truck similar to the car I had traveled in between Kassel and Cologne. (It was called a *Lieferwagen*, meaning delivery vehicle.) I expressed interest in it and learned it cost several thousand marks less than the cars I'd been looking at. But it had already been sold.

The salesman said he had another truck out back, so we went to look at it. This one was white and decorated along the side with blue stripes and the sunburst logo of Hertie, a now defunct department store. White was preferable to brown anyway.

I knew I might be taking a chance buying a used delivery truck because of all the wear and tear, but I thought it might be more practical than a car. It had a relatively low 22,000 km on it (13,750 miles) and cost 5,000 DM ($1,800 at the time), which was just about what I had in the bank.

I expected a lot of red tape, but buying it was surprisingly simple. While I picked up the money, the dealer took care of the tax, license and registration. I returned five days later and exchanged five 1,000 mark notes for the keys. I had asked that the Hertie logo, which was stuck on with adhesive, be removed, but I kept the stripes to give the truck a little character.

Even though I had driven rental cars a few times, I was

reluctant to drive off the lot and into traffic because I knew how aggressive the German drivers were. But I gritted my teeth and did it. It didn't take more than a few blocks to feel comfortable. Someone had warned me it would be hard to get used to the gearshift lever protruding from the dashboard, but since I was used to driving stick shift cars, that was no problem at all.

I never did test drive the thing, so I was back at the dealer within a week to get the wheels aligned, a problem that naturally wasn't covered by the limited warranty.

Getting a driver's license was remarkably easy. According to regulations at the time, any foreign resident who had been in Germany for less than one year could get one simply by going to his local city hall (*Rathaus*), showing his existing license, filling out a form, handing over an ID photo and paying a token fee. I got a license in no time.

Anyone who waited longer than a year had to attend a driving school, or *Fahrschule,* which cost a small fortune, plus take a difficult written exam which was given only in German.

Mary Beth waited beyond a year. But when she finally went in to get her license, she deftly managed to direct the clerk's attention to the newest stamp in her passport indicating she had only recently arrived in Germany. It worked.

Unlike the USA, where periodic renewals are required, a German license was good for life. That meant the photo on virtually every license showed the driver as a teenager, unless he or she waited until later in life to apply.

That changed in the late 90s when Germans had the option of getting European Union licenses, necessitating new photos. Still, there were some German pensioners who stuck with their original licenses, some of which were old enough to be decorated with swastikas.

Parking was at a premium in Germany, especially at the *Deutsche Welle.* Under the building were two levels of parking with room for hundreds of cars. But there were far more cars with little blue parking stickers on the windshields than there were parking spaces, and parking on nearby streets was virtually impossible. Almost any hour of the workday, cars were lined up at the entrance to the garage, waiting for someone to leave. During business hours, a guard in a glass booth would regulate access. I always wondered what kind of excuse the drivers who waited forever gave when they showed up late for work or took an unbelievably long lunch.

I was lucky. I got a parking sticker. Since I walked to work and didn't want to leave the truck on the street in front of the apartment, I usually left it in the garage, hidden away in the darkest recesses. I always feared one of those people hungry for a parking space might notice it was always there and put a nasty note on my windshield, but it never happened.

The Neanderthal incident

Peter bought a car long before I did. One Sunday he and Lone invited me to ride along on an outing to Neandertal, the area near Düsseldorf where the skeleton of the Neanderthal Man was discovered in 1856.

In German, *Tal* is the word for valley. The skeleton was found in a valley where a 17th century poet named Joachim Neander went to relax. The area later became known as the Neander Valley or Neandertal.

There was a museum near the grotto where the 60,000 year-old bones were found. In the gift shop, one of the souvenirs was a circular bumper sticker measuring about three inches in diameter which featured the face of the Neanderthal Man. Printed along the edge, it said, *"Ich bin Neandertal,"* meaning, "I am a Neanderthal."

I immediately thought of Rex and bought a sticker to put on the front of his desk.

After we got back to work, Peter and I did just that while Rex was out of the office. The secretary later told us

Rex freaked out when he spotted it. We had a million laughs as we imagined him turning into a real Neanderthal.

On the job

The best thing about *European Journal* was that there was nothing routine about it. Every day was different.

Peter, Mary Beth and I would do any number of shoots per month, being away from the office anywhere from half a day to a week. We traveled almost everywhere in Europe. There was no such thing as a typical month. I might spend two separate days on shoots somewhere in Germany, one day in Amsterdam and three days in Paris. Another month it might be one day each in Belgium, Switzerland and the Netherlands, plus three days in London.

We didn't have an assignment editor. Although Rendelsmann would occasionally hand us a project, we were responsible for coming up with our own ideas. We were free to do whatever we wanted providing we could get Rendelsmann's OK. If we wanted to go to a certain country or cover a certain topic, we presented our ideas, got them approved and off we went.

In order to get approval, we had to fill out a form for Rendelsmann summarizing our plans. Once we got his OK, we contacted one office to arrange for a camera crew, another to get information on planes, trains and hotels if necessary, and a third to request any video we might need. We could order video of almost anything, old or new, from the German TV networks, *ARD* and *ZDF*.

It was easy to keep up with the latest visuals. Every evening an intern would record all the German news programs and type out a brief description of each story. Anyone could consult the list for ideas. That's where Rex found the *Dups*.

Sometimes I'd run into a brick wall, like trying to get a clip of Jesse Owens winning gold for the United States in the 1936 Berlin Olympics. The legendary Leni Riefenstahl, who filmed the games, wanted considerably more than the *Deutsche Welle* would pay.

When I needed visuals for a story about the chemical weapons talks, I knew there wouldn't be any film from World War One, so I requested still photos. I got lucky. The archives contained a shot of two horses pulling a wagon carrying some officers. Each horse was wearing a gas mask. That became my opening shot.

We had to follow certain guidelines on hotel prices. For example, 120 DM a day ($45 to $50, depending on the exchange rate) was fine in London or Paris, but 80 DM was the limit in an out-of-the-way town. I learned that the hard way when the folks in the travel office went crazy after I spent 100 DM in a smaller German city.

We flew coach but traveled first class by rail.

After completing a story, we had to fill out a *Dienstreiseantrag,* or business travel form, so we could get per diem. As with hotels, there were different reimbursement rates for each city depending on how expensive it was. We got lunch money if we were out of the building for at least four hours.

On rare occasions, Rendelsmann would announce we were short of money and nobody could travel any farther than Bonn. But somehow they always pulled money out of a hat a few weeks later and the travel restriction was lifted.

When we weren't on the road, we were in the office writing, editing or chasing down new stories. I almost always wrote the first draft of my scripts by hand on a legal pad in the apartment where there were no distractions, then typed them onto a prompter form at the office.

We usually had an *Assistent* or *Assistentin* in the office. That's a university student who worked for a few months helping us do research and set up appointments, someone who'd be called an intern in the U.S. We didn't have computers yet, so one of the things the interns did was gather background material for us from the *DW* archives, mostly clippings from German magazines and newspapers with a few articles in French and English thrown in.

Peter, Mary Beth and I weren't the only reporters. Rex and Kathleen were among a handful of freelancers who occasionally shot stories.

Another contributor was prematurely bald Mark Rossman, an Oregonian who covered stories, wrote *Dup*s and directed the show when Belless wasn't there. Mark obviously wasn't going anywhere anytime soon because he was paying the mortgage on a house in the suburbs where he lived with his German wife and young son.

Other freelancers included Michael Riedner, Steve Smith and Cheryl Korman. Michael was a German from Nuremberg. He had lived in the United States as a child and spoke English well. Steve and Cheryl, both Americans, translated scripts from German and narrated them.

Cheryl, who was from Florida, occasionally shot stories too. She spoke fluent German, French and Spanish and often worked at conferences as a simultaneous translator.

Although Steve was a good narrator, his main job was writing articles for several U.S. newspapers. When he worked for us, he never covered any stories or appeared on camera, maybe because he had a few teeth missing and often needed a shave. A nice face for radio, as the saying goes.

One of the most unusual staff members was photographer Klaus von Koller, a huge man with a matted beard and hair who resembled a derelict Santa Claus. He always looked as if he had slept in the back of his Volvo station wagon. Depending on where we were headed, he would often have the assistant and soundman load up the gear at the *Deutsche Welle*, then meet us at an autobahn rest stop instead of coming to the office.

Klaus enjoyed alcohol. He once ruined a story in Paris after he had a few drinks and got confused about whether the camera was on or off. We were shooting a piece about a soul food restaurant that had a black American chef. After interviewing him as he started preparing the basics, we had to wait an hour for the restaurant to open so the customers would start coming in, and we did our waiting at the bar. Hurry up and wait was a part of almost every shoot.

The finished tape had moving shots of chair legs and the floor as the camera was carried from one spot to another. As soon as the picture was set up, the camera clicked off.

Naturally I wasn't happy about losing the story. I complained to Rendelsmann and gave him the field tape, but I don't know if he ever looked at it. The staff photographers had what amounted to lifetime jobs, so there wasn't much Rendelsmann could do anyway.

I have to give Klaus credit for one classic line. We once shot part of a story in a room above a London pub, wrapping up at 11 a.m. just as the pub was opening. Klaus was at the bar downing a pint as the camera assistant said, "Hey Klaus, I thought you never drank before noon." Saluting with his mug, Klaus replied, "It's noon in Germany!"

Legoland, the Pied Piper and gingerbread cookies

European Journal dealt with almost every subject imaginable. Most of the focus was on international relations, primarily relations between various European countries and the United States. Also high on the list were social topics, business and economics, medical stories including AIDS, plus politics and the environment.

We all did feature stories now and then. Peter reported on Legoland in Denmark and Mary Beth went to the medieval town of Hamelin for a story on the famous Pied Piper.

One of my lighter pieces was about the quaint Belgian town of Dinant, which is known for its Christmas cookies. As the story goes, Dinant was under siege back in 1466. The only foods left were flour and honey, so the people made a dough and baked it, producing crude gingerbread cookies. The town was saved from starvation and the cookies became a tradition.

Even today, the recipe is the same, nothing but flour and honey. I tried making it myself. The cookies were as tough as the sole of a shoe, but it worked.

Dinant also was the home of Adolphe Sax (1814-1894) who invented – guess what? – the saxophone.

My most infamous story was about a platoon of specially equipped motorcycles that roamed the boulevards of Paris scooping up dog doo. There were more dogs per capita in Paris than any other European city, but only seven percent of the land was devoted to parks, and some were off limits to dogs. The result was 20 tons of canine pollution each day, most of it in the wrong places.

Working with a freelance photographer, we got a one-in-a-million shot of a dog casually walking into a café to illustrate what a pampered life they led.

The star of the story was one of the 75 motorcycles and its state-of-the-art pooper scooper, which we filmed in action. After the offensive matter was spotted, the driver lowered a special arm onto it, then a jet of water blasted it off the pavement and a powerful vacuum sucked it into a sealed tank.

Tourists and natives alike were so fascinated that some stopped to snap photos. Despite being attention-grabbers, the motorcycles barely put a dent in the problem.

Peter concentrated on Scandinavia and occasionally traveled to Italy. He once remarked that the smartest thing his grandfather ever did was leave Italy.

Although Mary Beth often covered women's issues, one of her more unusual pieces was about an ultra right-wing gathering whose participants were thinly disguised neo-Nazis. I kidded her about it, asking if she had won the Eva Braun Look-Alike Contest – Eva being Hitler's longtime companion, last-minute wife – or been chosen Miss Death Head or *Totenkopf,* the name for the skull and crossbones insignia.

Of course, it's against the law in Germany to be a Nazi or deny the Holocaust happened.

I became acquainted with the various European branches of government by covering the European Union executive committee in Brussels, the European Parliament in Strasbourg and the European Court of Justice in Luxembourg, plus the conventional weapons negotiations in Vienna and the chemical weapons talks in Geneva. Although much of the subject matter was dry, it was always interesting to meet the people and see the places that were often in the news.

I occasionally wound up doing stories about things I'd never heard of before but should have. One was a protest movement backed by middle-aged churchgoers that helped prevent the deployment of Cruise missiles in the Netherlands. Another was Britain's Farnborough Air Show, where my press pass allowed me to check out the newest aircraft from around the world while sampling goodies from lavish buffet tables.

Doing a piece on arms dealers, legal and illegal, I learned that anyone with the right money could buy anything from a World War One machine gun to a new jet fighter or a reconditioned submarine. The biggest exporter of weapons at the time was the Soviet Union, with other countries such as Egypt and Brazil getting into the act, lured by easy money. Large transactions, I was told, were only possible with government backing.

When asked about the morality of their business, arms dealers said all weapons are defensive and they were only helping countries deal with feelings of insecurity.

A story about the smuggling of articles made from animals on the endangered species list gained me entry into a basement storeroom at Frankfurt International Airport.
An eerie array of stuffed animals, birds, reptiles and other creatures was kept on shelves until the smugglers went to trial. I was surprised to see many items made from turtles.

Although hundreds of items passed through that room each year, customs agents said the number had been declining, presumably because the smugglers knew they might get caught.

I visited the headquarters of the World Wildlife Fund near Geneva to get an interview for the story. Although the WWF was especially concerned about the poaching of rhino horns because the rhinoceros was being wiped out, officials said an even greater threat was the destruction of habitat by an expanding human population, especially in Africa.

I tried to make it to Britain once a year, partly to get back in touch with the English language by catching shows at the reasonably priced theaters and prowling the book shops. My first trip there was by car with a *Hausteam* after I'd been on the Continent for nearly a year. As we left the ferry after crossing the channel, I was amazed I could read all the billboards alongside the road.

The only thing I disliked about working in Britain was that people I interviewed often asked for money. That always annoyed me because I had never run into that anywhere else and I hated negotiating. It was never a lot of money, maybe £25, but just the fact that they did it was irritating. With the *Deutsche Welle's* blessing, I listed the contributions on my expense account as donations. My guess is the practice may have been started by the intensely competitive tabloid newspapers.

D-Day +40

Somehow I became *European Journal's* unofficial military correspondent. That was fine because I enjoyed those kind of stories.

In the spring of 1984, Herr Rendelsmann assigned me to do a preview of the 40th anniversary of the Normandy invasion. It was a great idea. I wish I'd thought of it.

Rendelsman suggested I contact the *Bundesarchiv,* or federal archive, to get D-Day film shot by the German military. The archive was housed in an old fortress overlooking Koblenz, a city built at the confluence of the Rhine and Moselle rivers, about one hour south of Cologne. I made an appointment, then traveled there by train and taxi.

I was led into a dimly lit room equipped with a table for viewing 35 mm film. I requested footage from the 4th, 5th and 6th of June. What I got was the *Wochenschau* (Weekly Show), the newsreel shown in German theaters during the war. Each reel was laid flat on a spool, then hand-cranked through a viewer.

It was fascinating to watch the World War Two footage, noting that German casualties were never shown. The suspense grew as I put on the reel for June 6th. Unfortunately all I saw was a few seconds of ships on the horizon that may have had nothing to do with the invasion. Either the photographers had run for their lives or the Propaganda Ministry decided not to show the invasion. There was nothing I could use.

Back at the office, I got on the phone and tracked down the appropriate department at the Pentagon. About two weeks later, a video showing the D-Day invasion arrived. It was perfect because it combined both U.S. and German footage.

I shot the story with a *Hausteam,* traveling to Normandy in a company car. It was an eight hour drive. I had gone there on my own in a rental car a few weeks earlier, so I had a rough idea where everything was.

We only had two days to shoot the story because the *Deutsche Welle* was always trying to hold down expenses. As usual, we had to work as fast as we could, but try to give the piece the look of a documentary.

We filmed at the seaside town of Arromanches, where the Allies constructed an artificial harbor by sinking concrete docks that had been towed over from England; Pointe du Hoc, where President Reagan later saluted the U.S. Rangers who scaled a cliff to knock out a heavily fortified German position; and the American Military Cemetery, which was laid out on a bluff above Omaha Beach. We were cautioned not to shoot grave markers where names might be visible.

We also visited the church at St. Mere Eglise where a U.S. paratrooper got hung up on the steeple before dawn on June 6th. Because of the depiction of that incident in the book and film *The Longest Day,* it was one of the most visited churches in France.

As we shot in and around German bunkers, I wondered what the members of the film crew were thinking, since their side had been on the losing end of the battle as well as the war.

On Omaha Beach, I interviewed Howard Gillingham, an Iowan who had landed on June 9th as a tank mechanic. A *European Journal* contact in Paris had tracked him down for me. A husky man of average height, Gillingham had returned to Normandy after the war, married a French woman and settled down in Le Molay Littry, a village not far from the beach. We met at the village café, which he and his wife had inherited. There wasn't enough room for him in our packed station wagon, so he volunteered to drive the two of us to the beach in his rickety old car.

Gillingham, who was 62 at the time, took us to the spot where he had come ashore. As Walter Cronkite and General Dwight Eisenhower had done 20 years earlier, we talked while walking along the beach. I wasn't trying to copy Cronkite. That was simply the best way to do the interview.

Gillingham said there was a lot of activity in 1944, but it was well organized and everyone seemed to know what he was doing. He pointed out that the Allies had built a large prisoner of war camp on a hill above the beach to discourage bombing by the Germans. He said he didn't think much about the invasion unless he was at the beach. He got misty-eyed when he described the scene. "You couldn't imagine the ships," he said. "All you could see was ships."

Of course there's much more to Normandy than reminders of D-Day, and it became one of my favorite getaway spots. It's the home of Camembert cheese as well as a powerful apple brandy called Calvados. The wide range of attractions in the province includes the city of Rouen in the east, where Joan of Arc was burned at the stake in 1431, to the incomparable Mont St. Michel in the west. The ancient coastal fortress, which is capped by an 11th century abbey, is undoubtedly one of the greatest sights in the world.

Mr. Gillingham told me that living near Mont St. Michel was just like living near Disneyland. Whenever relatives came to town, he had to take them there.

A few miles inland from Arromanches and the landing beaches is Bayeux, famous as the home of the Bayeux Tapestry, a strip of embroidered linen more than 200 feet long and about 20 inches wide that tells the story of the Norman Conquest. One joker described it as the world's longest tablecloth.

The resort town of Deauville has been a playground for the rich and famous since the 1860s. In addition to a nice beach, there's a casino, smart shops, a horse racing track and an annual film festival. Deauville was one of the settings for the 1966 film *A Man and a Woman*.

A short drive to the east is the picturesque little port of Honfleur, which has attracted artists since the days of the Impressionists.

Several ports in Normandy and Brittany serve as gateways to the British Channel Islands. From Carteret, north of Mont St. Michel, I made daytrips twice by hydrofoil to Jersey. It was a pleasant diversion – a bit of England plus duty free shopping just off the coast of France.

As a D-Day spinoff, I later did a story on U.S. military cemeteries in Europe. The one at Omaha Beach was only one of a dozen overseas cemeteries devoted to U.S. casualties from World War Two. Eight others date from the First World War. They are maintained by the American Battle Monument Commission, an independent agency created by Congress in 1923.

When American servicemen were killed in action, most were buried in makeshift graves where they fell. After the war, about two-thirds of the bodies were shipped back to the United States at the request of relatives. The others were consolidated into permanent resting places overseas.

For my story, I focused on a cemetery near the village of Henri Chapelle in the rolling green pastures of eastern Belgium. A total of 7,989 soldiers and airmen rest there, many of them killed in the Battle of the Bulge. There were 94 unknowns and 32 cases in which brothers were lying side-by-side. In one instance, three brothers were buried together.

Sixteen men tended the grounds year round.

I was impressed by the fact that although the cemetery was out of the way, one million people had visited during the previous year, including 76,000 Americans.

There were flowers at the base of many grave markers. The superintendent explained that some were placed there by people living nearby who had "adopted" certain servicemen. I found that to be very touching.

Holding hands in Verdun

A few months after Normandy, Rendelsmann dispatched me to Verdun in northeastern France to cover an historic meeting between French President François Mitterrand and German Chancellor Helmut Kohl.

Verdun was the famous meat grinder of World War One where French and German forces were locked in combat from February through November of 1916. The Germans captured several French forts in the first weeks. But when it was all over 10 months later, both sides were back where they started and as many as 200,000 troops were dead or missing. Another half million had been wounded.

The date of the Mitterrand-Kohl meeting was September 22, 1984. It was arranged that I would drive to

Verdun in my truck and meet up with a freelance cameraman based in Mainz.

Since it was a four hour drive, I left my apartment at 5 a.m. I figured it wouldn't be worth the trouble to find a dog-sitter, so Mr. Sluggo rode along. When I arrived in Verdun, I parked outside city hall where the press center was and took Sluggo for a quick walk. Then I found the cameraman and we picked up our credentials. There was no danger that Sluggo would be roasted in the truck because the skies were overcast and there was a light drizzle.

Mitterrand and Kohl began by paying their respects at two cemeteries, one French and one German. They traveled from spot to spot by helicopter, with the news media following in cars and vans. There was a mad scramble every time they changed locations.

At one point, a station wagon belonging to a French TV network lurched away with the tailgate open and the sound recorder bounced onto the road. I couldn't help but wonder if they got it working again. Actually, there was plenty of time because the whole thing was intended as a photo op anyway.

The dramatic moment came in front of the Ossuary, a large building which serves as a depository for the bones of 130,000 war dead. As a band played each country's anthem, Kohl and Mitterrand stood side-by-side in the drizzle holding hands. Photos of that moment came to symbolize the postwar reconciliation between France and Germany.

Dresden +40

Another war-related assignment took me to Dresden in February of 1985 to cover the 40th anniversary of the fire-bombing.

Dresden was deep inside East Germany, not far from the Czechoslovak border. The Communist state was officially known as the *Deutsche Demokratische Republik* (German Democratic Republic), or by its initials, *DDR*.

Of course there was nothing democratic about the *DDR*. From the end of the war until 1949, when Germany was split in two, the eastern part had been the Soviet zone of occupation. After East Germany built a wall around the western part of Berlin in 1961, the Allied-controlled zones in the city could only be reached by certain land and air corridors from West Germany.

During the Cold War, Lufthansa was barred from flying between West Germany and West Berlin. Only Allied military planes and commercial flights operated by the United States, France and Britain were allowed to fly the air corridors. Lufthansa didn't resume its Berlin flights until October, 1990, shortly after Germany was officially reunified.

I began my trip to Dresden by flying to West Berlin, where I met up with a freelance photographer named Manfred Strastil and his girlfriend/assistant Eva.

Strastil was thin with light brown curly hair, beady eyes and a ski jump nose. Eva was pleasant-looking with long dark hair and a pale complexion.

Since they were Berliners and I was a foreigner, we had to enter East Berlin through different gates. They dropped me off at Checkpoint Charlie, then drove to another entrance. I went through the passport check, then stood on the sidewalk for a while outside a nearby restaurant. It was very cold, so I stepped inside the outer door and asked if I could wait there. They said no, but I stayed anyway until Strastil drove up.

From there we headed to Dresden. Unlike West Germany, drivers had to be very careful not to exceed the speed limit because the *Vopos* (short for *Volkspolizei* or People's Police) were eager to fine anyone for speeding.

The autobahn seemed as if it hadn't been repaired since the war. As we traveled along avoiding the potholes, we could see the *Vopos* on the side of the road pointing radar guns at us from their junky little Trabant cars, which were partially hidden under military camouflage nets.

The Trabants had plastic bodies that were said to

splinter in an accident and two-stroke engines that belched smoke because, like some lawn mowers, oil had to be mixed in with the gas.

Once in Dresden, we checked into a hotel on one of the major streets. The entire street was lined with huge box-like buildings that all looked the same. Call it *DDR* Modern.

Before leaving the West, I changed 10 DM into Ostmark (east marks) because I could get 10 Ostmark for one DM, whereas the official exchange rate was one-to-one. I was stuck with the money because there was nothing to buy. I spent only 10 Pfennig (pennies) while I was there, buying a little paper *DDR* flag in a department store.

I had hoped to blow the money on food but Strastil insisted on paying for my dinner. I didn't know if he was just being nice or it was a sly way of padding his expense account. Although the *Deutsche Welle* knew about the availability of the cheap Ostmark, the company respected the official exchange rate. That meant Strastil could have written off 50 DM for a five DM meal.

It was easy to cut costs on meals with the Ostmark, but the East Germans weren't stupid. The hotel bill had to be paid with hard currency or a credit card.

The bombing of Dresden has come to be regarded as one of the more senseless episodes of the war. Long known as the "Florence of the Elbe," Dresden was famous for its baroque and rococo architecture which made the city itself an artistic treasure. Partly because of that, it had remained virtually untouched by the war.

That was until the night of February 13, 1945 when waves of British bombers swept over the city dropping 26,000 tons of explosives including incendiaries. The result was a firestorm that sucked oxygen from the air and generated temperatures up to 1,000 degrees. American planes followed with two smaller daylight raids.

No one knows how many people were killed.

Estimates range from 35,000 to 135,000 or more. The death toll was hard to determine because the city's population was swelled with tens of thousands of refugees who were fleeing Soviet troops advancing from the east. As the dead were pulled from the shattered buildings, bodies were stacked in the streets like cords of wood.

At the time of the raids, it was said Dresden had been attacked because it was a communications center. Some believed the purpose of the raid was to wear down the morale of the German people, although it was clear the war was grinding to a close. Most historians now agree that the firebombing was probably a political move, a case of British Prime Minister Winston Churchill trying to impress the Soviets.

Although there were still huge open spaces where there had once been narrow streets, a number of buildings had been meticulously reconstructed. The gala reopening of the opera house, which was gutted during the bombing, was timed to coincide with the anniversary. Reporters and photographers were allowed inside a few hours before the ceremony. It seemed strange that everything was new and even smelled new but was made to look 100 years old.

The East German government arranged for me to interview a woman who survived the attacks. We talked in a parking lot where her house had stood. She said she realized that war is war and she harbored no hate for any nation.

As another element of the story, I later traveled to a British military base in West Germany to interview a navigator who had been in one of the bombers. He said most of the airmen viewed Dresden as just another target.

One of the events we covered was a memorial service at dawn at a cemetery on the outskirts of the city. The temperature was below freezing and I had to stand in one spot for an hour shuffling my feet as a band played mournful songs. At least Strastil and Eva got to walk around with the camera.

The highlight was a wreath laying ceremony, known in German as a *Kranzniederlegung*, a good example of a *Schlangenwort* or snake word.

Even though we were there for an hour, the ceremony ran only 10 seconds in the finished piece. But that's pretty much how it usually worked out.

One of the first things I did when I got back to Cologne was buy sheepskin-lined boots so my toes would never get frosted again. Actually, it seldom got that cold in Cologne. The weather there could be described as temperate because of the influence of the English Channel – never too hot in the summer or too cold in the winter although ice and snow occasionally made an appearance.

The last POWs

The last prisoners of war from World War Two weren't released until 10 years after the war. That's because the Soviet Union had been holding more than 9,600 German POWs in retribution for Hitler's aggression. They were finally freed in 1955 at the urging of West German Chancellor Konrad Adenauer.

I have to confess I knew nothing about that until I was sent to cover a POW reunion at Bad Godesberg, the upscale Bonn suburb that was home to most of the embassies before the German capital was moved back to Berlin.

The group, called the German Homecoming Union, had 270,000 members in Germany and was affiliated with other prisoner of war societies in Europe. The annual meetings were held in different countries on a rotating basis.

Six-thousand people attended the gathering. Although most were German, other participants came from Austria, France, Italy, Belgium, Finland and Luxembourg.

Tents were set up and signs were hung here and there listing the names of prisons so it would be easier for people to find long lost friends. Lunch was served from a military-style field kitchen. The reunion was short on speeches and long on camaraderie.

I asked a man from Berlin what the former prisoners talked about. "We talk about life," he said. "And the fact that we're lucky to be alive. We talk about how the world should be, how it needs freedom, peace and trust instead of war."

Another man told me, "No one knows war better than a former POW and no one appreciates peace more."

The wall

"The kids ask why it's there. How do you answer them?"
– A West Berlin woman commenting on the wall.

East Germany, Berlin and the wall were constant sources of good stories.

There were actually two walls. One divided East Germany from West Germany, stretching 870 miles from the Baltic Sea to the Czechoslovak border. The other encircled West Berlin. If you picture East Germany as an oblong doughnut, West Berlin would be a small hole in the middle.

For one story, my photographer and I flew along a rural section of the wall in a *Bundesgrenzschutz* (Federal Border Protection) helicopter. It was easy to see why escape was difficult. There were at least half a dozen obstacles including two fences, sections of which were equipped with automatic firing devices, plus guard towers and bunkers, anti-vehicle ditches and, in remote areas, guard dogs.

Although the wall was put there to keep the East Germans at home, the Communist government called it the "anti-fascist wall" and pretended it was to prevent West Germany from attacking.

Seventeen villages sitting on the border were divided by walls. Civilian informers on the eastern side notified police if any strangers appeared in town.

A 23-year-old former East German border guard told me the guards were given daily orders to shoot to kill. He said any guard who allowed someone to escape because he didn't shoot could be sent to prison for up to five years.

The border was sealed from 1961 to 1989 – an entire generation. In later years, fewer and fewer people escaped, mainly because the East Germans made it more and more difficult to even reach the wall.

Many of the easterners who did escape wound up in a large dormitory in West Berlin run by a group of Protestant churches. It housed about 140 people, both families and individuals. Refugees lived in rooms furnished with bunk beds for four or five months until they found jobs and apartments.

Newcomers expressed amazement at the wide variety of consumer goods that were available, especially in supermarkets. They also said they liked the fact that they could say anything they wanted without being arrested.

Adjusting to freedom wasn't easy. A psychiatrist I interviewed said some of the refugees developed a deep depression when they couldn't find work, and about one out of 10 needed clinical treatment.

As one woman who had recently arrived remarked, "We who have been brought up and educated in the East are used to having our lives organized and not being responsible for ourselves. In this context, life here is certainly different and there is some stress."

We photographed former East Germans attending night school, where they learned how to deal with everyday things such as credit and insurance. In the Communist state, credit was unknown and insurance was provided by the government.

The adjustment was worth it. A woman attending the class said, "It's very depressing when you're standing in front of the wall and crying, knowing you can't take that little step. When I came to the West, it was a great feeling of happiness."

A Berlin tour guide told me most non-German tourists were very naive about the wall. He said they would stare at the armed guards in their towers, then ask questions such as, "Are the East Germans allowed to come over to shop?"

West Berlin had a special status during the Cold War. In the interest of keeping the city populated, the federal government gave anyone who lived there a break on income tax. The city became a magnet for hippies and anarchists because men of draft age living there were exempt from military service.

The smile of espionage

Judging from all the books and movies about espionage, you'd think West Berlin was the Cold War spy capital of Europe, especially since the wall gave the city an underlying feeling of intrigue.

But British writer Chapman Pincher, author of *Their Trade is Treachery,* told me most of the spying went on in Brussels because that's where NATO was headquartered.

He said Bonn was the best place in Germany for espionage because it was the capital.

The most famous East German spy was Günter Guillaume, a mole who was sent to the West in the mid-50s and worked his way into a job as personal assistant to Chancellor Willy Brandt. His arrest in April of 1974 led to Brandt's resignation just 10 days later. Guillaume was sentenced to 13 years in prison but released in a spy swap after serving only six years.

His penetration of the Brandt government was the greatest achievement of East German spymaster Marcus Wolf, who also had success with lonely heart spies – men and women who preyed on diplomats seeking companionship, convincing them to hand over secrets.

A classic example would be an unmarried secretary

over the age of 30 working in a high government office. As a West German intelligence official explained, "It's better to buy the person with a key to the safe than blow it open."

About 20 lonely heart spies were uncovered in the 80s. Most fled to the East to avoid arrest. One who got caught and sent to prison was a 51-year-old woman who worked in the foreign affairs department of the president's office. She had been recruited by an East Bloc agent who wined and dined her. Over a 12 year period, she smuggled out 1,700 bits of secret information for the Soviet KGB.

In order to counteract that sort of thing, the West German Counterintelligence Agency distributed posters to government offices and defense contractors to alert them to the presence of lonely heart spies.

One poster showed a cute blonde with an enticing gaze. Down in one corner, it said, "The Smile of Espionage?" Another warned that love affairs are sometimes planned in East Berlin and the partner is already married – to the East German security service.

Some of the posters included a phone number to call if anyone had tips on possible spies. People did call.

I later did a story about the John F. Kennedy School in Berlin which specializes in bilingual education – teaching English-speaking students to be fluent in German and German students to be fluent in American English. Visiting one class of German teenagers, I was amazed at how flawless their English was. Although they looked like Germans because of their dress, they had perfected the American accent. That is, until I directed the conversation to World War Two and one girl pronounced Hitler as Heet-lah. She apparently wasn't familiar with the American pronunciation, so the German pronunciation dropped in. If that had happened in the early 1940s and she had been a Nazi spy, that slip of the tongue would have been a dead giveaway – recalling the mistake made in the 1964 James Garner film *36 Hours*.

Police, police!

I was working in London with a British camera crew and one of our stories took us on a drug raid.

It was a long day. We had already shot parts of two other stories before we met with detectives in the early evening. They were all in plain clothes and typical of any police you might see in TV dramas.

After a briefing at the police station, we set off in several vehicles to the working class neighborhood of Brixton in southwest London. The cameraman, his assistant and I were in a large police van. We parked across the street from a block of three-story row houses as police watched people go in and out of one of the buildings. It was a summer night and it was stifling inside the van.

After an hour, the police decided to move. We all jumped out and ran to the house, then charged through the door and up a stairway. First in line were two detectives who were yelling, "Police, police!" The cameraman and his assistant were next, then me, then more police. It was quite exhilarating not knowing what was on the other side of the door, whether someone might start shooting.

Inside was a group of hippies who could have come straight from Central Casting. The head man resembled Charles Manson but wasn't nearly as evil-looking. There were a couple of other young men and a French woman with long dishwater blonde hair.

In one room was a homemade wire cage measuring at least two cubic yards. It contained several snakes, some possibly venomous. Police asked the hippies to remove the snakes so they could search for drugs. They didn't find any.

Detectives flipped over a mattress lying on a box spring on the floor and picked up a fist-sized roll of British pounds. They also discovered a pipe tobacco tin containing hallucinogenic mushrooms. When they asked the woman if she had ever seen them before, she replied dreamily, "Yes, I've seen some in the forest."

Police found marijuana and LSD but no heroin. The Manson look-alike was charged with selling drugs and the rest were freed.

Back at the station, the police admitted they hadn't expected the raid to result in a major bust. If they had, they wouldn't have taken us along because their case might have been jeopardized in court by the presence of the camera.

Later, when I started putting the piece together in Cologne, I thought the conversations between the police and hippies were so riveting that I didn't want to cover them with narration. I wrote an opening paragraph to set up the story, then let the actuality roll, interspersed with sound bites from drug experts. I wrapped up the story with a closing paragraph.

Rex went nuts. He insisted I write a script to cover the conversations. I appealed to Rendelsmann for support as Rex complained, "We can see stuff like that on TV every night."

Rendelsmann echoed my feelings when he countered by saying, "Yes, but this is real."

I had read that one of the more interesting things to do in London was visit the Old Bailey Criminal Court to watch a trial in progress.

I turned up there on one of my non-working visits to the city only to be disappointed. The first letdown came when I was ushered into the gallery in one of the modern courtrooms. I had expected something old and quaint.

Secondly, the proceedings opened with a request that the clerk read back certain testimony from the previous day. No one was permitted to enter or leave the gallery while the court was in session, so I and a dozen or more other spectators got to listen to the clerk reading for most of the morning. I escaped as soon as I could.

Although cocaine was popular in the United States in the mid-80s, heroin was the drug of choice in Europe because it was cheaper. But the new crack cocaine was making inroads.

Amsterdam was always a good source for stories about drugs because of public tolerance toward soft drugs. Stepping off the train at the Central Station, you could often catch a whiff of marijuana before you hit the street.

The city had been known as the drug mecca of Europe since 1976 when the government lowered the penalties for soft drugs. Although even soft drugs were technically illegal, the government reasoned they couldn't be eliminated, so why not permit limited use of them? Soon hundreds of so-called coffee shops opened up selling small quantities of marijuana and hashish.

The problem was that Amsterdam's liberal reputation attracted hard drug users and the sale of heroin and cocaine became more brazen despite harsh penalties. Many addicts turned to robbery and assault to finance their habit. Crime went up.

Amsterdam residents learned to leave nothing in their cars for fear of attracting thieves. Nevertheless, addicts broke the windows to steal the radios. On almost any side street, you could see a pile of beaded glass indicating a car had been vandalized.

The owner of a large auto glass company told me half the windows he replaced were smashed during break-ins. One young man waiting for a new window said his attitude was definitely changing.

The public gradually became less tolerant of the junkies, as the Dutch called them. In one high-crime area, a woman I interviewed said the residents used to feel sorry for the junkies but their tolerance gradually turned to irritation. Shopkeepers in the neighborhood broadcast recorded warnings over loudspeakers telling shoppers to watch out for pickpockets. They also hired two plainclothes guards to patrol their street.

Reacting to the growing discontent, authorities shut down coffee shops where hard drugs were sold and started deporting foreign drug offenders. They also supplemented their methadone program with a strictly controlled heroin handout to wean the junkies of their habit.

The Netherlands also had a very liberal attitude toward the sale of sex. Prostitution was legal and Amsterdam's main red light district, where hookers displayed their attributes in gaudy storefront windows, was one of the hottest nighttime tourist attractions in the city.

Hookers were the farthest thing from my mind when I drove to Amsterdam early one Saturday morning to play tourist for the day.

Since parking was nearly impossible anywhere in the city center, I left the truck some blocks away and started walking. Crossing one of the many bridges spanning the canals, I spotted an ordinary-looking young woman standing along the rail holding a cardboard cup of coffee in her right hand and a doughnut in her left. As I drew near, she asked if I wanted to go with her. I politely declined.

Apparently I'd been walking right through the red light district and didn't know it.

It was truly surreal being propositioned at eight o'clock in the morning by a woman standing on a bridge munching a doughnut.

Good old Amsterdam.

The flood

It seemed as if whenever Rendelsmann wanted a story done immediately, he gave it to me. One day I was at my desk when he called and told me to meet a camera crew at the back door in 20 minutes. I was going to do a story on "the flood."

I told him I didn't have a necktie. He said, "Do it anyway."

The Rhine was running about 30 feet above normal in some places, producing the worst flooding in 70 years.

The camera crew and I went to Rodenkirchen, the first

suburb south of Cologne, to shoot the damage and interview people who had been flooded out. In a neighborhood where narrow streets sloped down to the river, a man who was bailing out his bar told us, "In the 18th century, this probably happened once. In the 19th century, twice. This century, maybe four or five times. It's very clear. We're restricting the river too much."

He was absolutely right. I later interviewed an expert on flood plain ecology who confirmed that the major cause of the flooding was flood control projects.

At least 40% of the Rhine had been artificially straightened or confined by dikes or dams, and when the water couldn't spread out, it rose.

Out of curiosity, I checked the Rhine near my apartment. Usually I could walk to the river and watch barges hauling freight between Rotterdam and Switzerland. But during the flood, there was no traffic whatsoever. The water was so high the barges couldn't possibly squeeze under the bridges.

On the other side of the river, several hundred yards away, soccer fields were completely submerged. Set way back from where the riverbank normally was, the clubhouse had water up to its windows.

On my side was a much higher bank topped with a waist-high stone wall, and the water crested only one inch from the top. The path where people did their Sunday afternoon strolls was under more than 20 feet of water. It was easy to sense the immense power of the river as it surged along the wall.

Adjustments

Shopping, European style

When I arrived in Germany, the biggest complaint of Americans living there was the inconvenient shopping hours. All stores, no matter what they sold, were closed every evening and most of the weekend.

They loosened up their hours in recent years with most staying open until 8 p.m. Monday through Friday and 10 p.m. on Saturday, but for a long time they closed at 6:30 on weekdays, 2 on Saturdays and never even thought of opening on Sundays.

With the 6:30 closing, it was like a shopping cart demolition derby when people working 9 to 5 crowded the supermarkets on their way home to pick up a few things. Saturdays were even worse unless you got to a store when it opened at 8 a.m. and got out as quickly as possible.

The principal supporters of the restricted hours were the German labor unions which believed longer hours would keep retail workers away from their families. Years ago, the unions even staged demonstrations against a government proposal to extend Saturday shopping hours.

Even today, most stores remain closed on Sundays across the Continent. There are two notable exceptions in Germany. Many bakeries open for a few hours in the morning and/or afternoon so people can buy pastries.

Also open are grocery stores located in major train stations. Those stores are permitted to sell provisions for travelers such as beer and sandwiches.

The Sunday closings don't keep Germans away from the downtown shopping areas. Many walk among the large department stores doing what's known as *Schaufenster-bummeln,* which means show window strolling – another example of a *Schlangenwort* or snake word.

Using Sunday as a day of rest may seem revolutionary to mall-crawling Americans, but after the initial shock, it's easy to get used to, especially if you're invited to *Kaffee und Kuchen* – coffee and cake – a very pleasant German version of afternoon tea.

Whenever I heard people complain about surly clerks in American stores, I imagined how surprised they'd be in Germany. Service seemed to be especially bad in department stores when I first arrived, with most clerks ignoring me. When I did get their attention, their attitude often seemed to be, "Why are you bothering me?"

Whenever I returned to the U.S., I was surprised by how nice the clerks were. It was a case of reverse culture shock. They almost seemed too friendly.

After I got my truck, I started shopping about once a month at a big supermarket on the outskirts of Liège in eastern Belgium, a drive of about one hour. I had seen the store from the highway while traveling through Belgium to shoot stories. I decided to check it out. It was called GB (Grand Bazaar) Maxi then, but was later bought out by the French chain Carrefour.

The store wasn't necessarily any cheaper than a German supermarket but was easier on the nerves. It was much larger, open a few hours longer, had many products that weren't available in Germany, including more U.S. brands, and more checkout lanes. It also had a restaurant where one could relax with a cup of coffee and a snack before heading home.

Whenever I visited France on my own, I'd try to stop at a *hypermarché* (giant supermarket) or *boulangerie* (bakery) and buy a baguette just before leaving the country. For some inexplicable reason, the French loaves always tasted better than baguettes made anywhere else, even right across the border in Belgium. I once got the bright idea of bringing French bread flour back to Cologne and baking it myself. No, it didn't have the *boulangerie* taste.

There was nothing wrong with German food. It was just kind of exotic to shop in Belgium and France.

Germany has excellent meats and sausages, a nice variety of cheeses, pastries to die for and fantastic bread. Rye bread or *Roggenbrot* was my favorite. I heard when Germans overseas are asked what they miss most about their country, many say the bread.

Although German beer is certainly among the best in the world – especially the local Cologne lager called *Kölsch* – I occasionally brought back a case of Heineken or Amstel from the Netherlands. Those beers were not available in Germany because they supposedly did not meet German purity standards. According to tradition, beer sold in Germany must contain only four ingredients – water, yeast, hops and barley – and most foreign beers were said to be loaded with extras. One of the foreign brands that qualified for sale in Germany was Guinness from Ireland.

What's in a name?

The German government did more than just make sure the citizens had quiet Sunday afternoons free of the hassles of shopping. When a child was born, the parents had to clear his or her name with the government to make sure it was acceptable. That's why you'd never meet a German named Moon Unit Schneider.

A new word: *Vorschuß*

The symbol that looks like a fancy capital B is called an esszet and it represents two s's. An example is *Straßenbahn* rather than *Strassenbahn*. Either is acceptable.

Germany may have the reputation for being well organized and efficient, but that wasn't necessarily so when it came to the *Deutsche Welle*.

One of the first problems Peter, Mary Beth and I ran into was getting paid.

In Germany, an employer automatically deposited a worker's salary into his bank account. But no money was turning up in ours. Instead of being paid each month, the company offered us a *Vorschuß,* or advance on our salary. We'd tell the payroll office how much we wanted and pick it up in cash at the cashier, or *Kasse*.

The story we got was that European Television Service had pulled a fast one by hiring us without telling the *Deutsche Welle*. The *Welle* apparently tried to solve the problem by not paying us, hoping we would disappear. Fortunately we had letters confirming two year contracts.

We were the only ones on the show with contracts. We were told the company was being very careful because a group of freelancers had sued for permanent jobs a while back and a court had ruled in their favor, forcing the company to hire hundreds of people it didn't want. The number was probably exaggerated but the story was true.

Rex was one of those people, a so-called lifetime freelancer. According to regulations, the only way to get rid of one was to reduce his workload by 10 % each year until he either quit in disgust or the job eventually evaporated.

After missing a few paychecks, we decided the best way to handle the matter was to join the union, the *RFFU,* so it could work on our behalf. *RFFU* stands for *Rundfunk-Fernseh-Film-Union,* which simply means Radio-Television-Film-Union.

The *RFFU* representative in the building told us if the *Deutsche Welle* didn't start paying us soon, the union lawyer would intervene. But that didn't work as well as we had hoped. As the weeks went by without anything happening, he kept telling us to wait just a little longer. We got so impatient that we gave up and hired our own lawyer. We tracked one down and all three of us went to see him in his office.

The lawyer sent a letter to the *Deutsche Welle* asking why we weren't being paid. We were put on the payroll immediately.

Then the lawyer sent us a bill. We handed it to the union rep. The union graciously paid.

Peter, Mary Beth and I thought the affair was all over until we simultaneously received registered letters from the lawyer demanding more money. He had also billed the *Deutsche Welle* and the company refused to pay, so he was trying to squeeze the money out of us.

We took the bills to the *RFFU*. The lawyer hadn't indicated what the charges were for, other than "services rendered." The union asked him to itemize. We never heard from him again.

Krankenversicherung

Initially there was some confusion over whether the *Deutsche Welle* would cover part of our health insurance, known as *Krankenversicherung*. It was a relief to find out that an employer was required by law to reimburse an employee for 50% of the premiums.

There were two categories of health insurance. If your salary was below a certain level, you were eligible for inexpensive government-subsidized insurance. If you were above that line, which we were, you had to get what was known as *privat* or private insurance.

I bought mine from a salesman who occasionally roamed the building seeking new clients. He was easy to deal with because he had lived in England and spoke perfect English. The insurance cost about $10 a day. That sounded shockingly expensive at first, but it wasn't bad considering the 50% company reimbursement and other rebates.

Here's how it worked: At the end of each year, the insurance company sent out a statement saying how much you had paid in premiums. You turned it in to the payroll office and the reimbursement was deposited into your bank account.

If the insured person didn't submit any bills, he or she could get a further rebate of up to four months of premiums. The insurance company would send out a letter at the beginning of each year telling the client how much his rebate would be. If doctor visits and prescriptions added up to less than the rebate, you could take the rebate. Do that for several years and you could get up to four months of premiums returned. Combine the 50% reimbursement and the rebates and you got a year's coverage for only two monthly payments.

Of course, if you had to go to a hospital or had big medical bills, the insurance would pay every penny, but you started over on the rebates.

Income tax or *Lohnsteuer*

There was no escaping income tax.

U.S. citizens working for German companies had to fill out both their 1040s and the German *Lohnsteuer* forms but were spared paying any U.S. taxes unless they were fairly well off. Foreign income up to $70,000 was excluded from taxation at that time and any taxes paid to Germany were deductible.

There were a number of differences between the two taxes. In Germany, instead of doing the calculations yourself, you filled in the numbers and employees at the *Finanzamt,* or finance office, did the math. That may sound simple, but many Germans hired a tax adviser known as a *Steuerberater* to find as many deductions as possible.

My girlfriend at the time, an Irish woman, knew a

German who did her taxes at a reasonable cost. He had worked for the British Forces and spoke English well, so I used him too.

Unlike the U.S., you could deduct the cost of any insurance payments, including car insurance, providing the policy was written in Germany. U.S. life insurance didn't count, but German life insurance did.

You could also deduct the cost of getting to work, writing off your monthly bus pass or the kilometers you drove. There was some cheating done on that. My tax man indicated I took the bus to work. Since I walked and preferred to be honest, I omitted that when I did the form in ink.

Writing wrongs

Writing German is very difficult, sometimes impossible, for people learning it as a second language. But not even Germans can seem to agree on how to write a simple letter. I discovered this when I needed help in dealing with the phone company, or *Fernmeldeamt.*

Today in Germany, if a customer requests it, the phone company will supply a list of all calls made, just as U.S. phone companies have done forever. When I first arrived in Cologne, the bill simply listed the number of "units" used. Some people bought little counters that hooked up to the phone and kept track of the units, but I never even considered that.

One month I received a bill for about 400 DM. I knew I had made more calls than usual, but I thought the bill should have been about half that amount.

I drafted a letter in German to ask the phone company for an explanation. Since my German was rather primitive, I asked my Irish friend who was fluent in the language to check it. She said, "Oh, no, no, no. That's all wrong."

She proceeded to rewrite it.

I thought the tone of her letter was too nasty, so I showed it to the Wissemanns a few days later. Their reaction was, "Oh, no, no, no. That's all wrong."

They rewrote it.

Just to make sure I had it right, I showed the new version to one of the executives at the *Deutsche Welle*. His reaction was, "Oh, no, no, no. That's all wrong."

He rewrote it. I trusted his opinion and didn't want to rewrite the letter forever, so I mailed it.

It seemed as if 100 Germans could have seen the letter and each one would have rewritten it, whereas in an English-speaking area, it probably would have been fine after the first touchup.

The phone company responded by asking me to fill out a form listing all the calls I'd made. I hadn't kept a record, but did the best I could from memory.

A few weeks later, a woman from the phone company called. She said they had made a mistake and would be refunding 68 DM. I had no idea how they reached their decision, but it was nice to get something back.

When answering the phone in Germany, it's customary to say your last name instead of hello. This is useful in getting rid of people who dial the wrong number. When they hear an unexpected name, they say, *"Tut mir leid,"* (Sorry) and hang up.

Urlaub

One of the big pluses of working in Germany was the liberal amount of vacation, known as *Urlaub*.

Anyone younger than 30 got 25 working days off. That's five whole weeks a year to start with. If you were 30 or over, you got 30 days. And that didn't count holidays and comp days. There are usually at least two weeks of holidays in Germany each year. Toss in a good amount of comp time and it was possible to get two months off.

Most Europeans, including the Germans, took their

vacations in summer. That often made it difficult to set up interviews because many people were not in their offices. That was also true at Christmas because many Europeans disappeared around the middle of December and didn't reappear until early January.

I had always heard virtually everyone in France went on vacation in August but found it hard to believe. Sure enough, I got to Paris once in August and streets that were normally giant parking lots, like the Champs Elysee, were nearly deserted.

Interlude

Pause

Autumn 1985. My two-year contract was drawing to a close and I had to figure out a way to hold on to the job. It would have been nice to have a new contract tacked onto the first one. But that wasn't possible because the *Deutsche Welle* believed that having two consecutive contracts would have put me or anyone else in a position to sue for a lifetime job. The only solution was a *Pause*.

That's the same as pause in English except it's pronounced POW-suh and it more or less means "take a break." It was one of the first words I learned at *Europa Kolleg*. When it was time for the hourly recess, the teacher would say, *"Pause, pause."*

Management said I'd have to take a *Pause* and disappear for at least six months before I could get another contract.

When Mary Beth and Peter finished their contracts a few weeks earlier, they each decided to start their own companies so they could continue reporting. That meant finding a European partner for legal reasons and creating a business on paper. In Peter's case, it was easy. Since his wife Lone was European, she became the partner. Mary Beth teamed up with a German woman who had lived in the U.S. and done some work with *European Journal*.

Each received a set payment per story. With it, they hired camera crews and editors, paid all travel expenses and pocketed what was left. I understand they could usually earn more than they had under their reporting contracts, especially if they held down costs by shooting several stories at the same location.

Fortunately everything fell into place for me without

having to start a business. Plans were quickly made for the next nine months, after which I would get a new two-year contract.

First, I spent time traveling with my father. Using a Soviet travel agency, I signed us up for a one-week package tour to Russia. For only 1,810 DM ($700) for both of us, we visited Leningrad (later renamed St. Petersburg) and Moscow with a group of Germans. The price included all transportation, hotel rooms and meals. Excursions cost extra.

We couldn't have asked for a better tour. We began by traveling by bus from the Cologne area to the East German city of Erfurt, where we caught a plane to Leningrad. After three days of sightseeing, which included a visit to the renowned Hermitage Museum of art and culture, we took a comfortable overnight train to Moscow, where we spent another three days before flying back to Erfurt. In each city we could either take part in organized outings such as the ballet or circus, or do whatever we wanted. The Russians fed us so well that I gained weight despite plenty of walking.

Following a short stay back in Cologne, we picked up a rental car and spent three weeks touring southern Europe, driving down the rugged Yugoslav coast to Greece, taking a ferry across to Italy, then traveling north through France and back to Germany. Mr. Sluggo stayed in a kennel while we were in Russia but joined us on the road trip.

It was very enjoyable, partly because my father preferred to stay in nice hotels, eat good meals and didn't mind picking up the bills.

For stage two, Transtel executives suggested I spend part of my time improving my German. With their assistance, I managed to get a scholarship for another month-long language course, this time at the highly respected Goethe Institute. The Institute, largely supported by the government, was set up after World War Two to promote the study of the

A Temporary European

German language and culture. It was named for Johann Wolfgang von Goethe, the greatest of Germany's classical writers. There were offices in 80 countries.

I had my choice of many locations. I choose the nearest, at Boppard – one of a string of small towns hugging the Rhein south of Koblenz – a place where Germans went for mini-vacations, attracted by cozy hotels and the opportunity for leisurely walks along the river.

I commuted from Cologne, driving down Sunday night and returning on Friday night. The trip took a little more than an hour, mostly on the autobahn.

Driving my little Renault truck in winter was always a chilling experience because there was too much interior space for the heater to heat and no insulation. Since the engine apparently was geared lower for stop-and-go delivery work, it seemed to strain when it was cruising at top speed on the autobahn – 120 kilometers per hour or 75 mph.

Boppard turned out to be a nice break from the job. For accommodation, another male student and I stayed on the ground floor of a modern split-level home owned by an older woman. We each had our own room, complete with kitchen facilities. We shared a bathroom. Mr. Sluggo was permitted in the house, so I took him along. Since it was December, it snowed occasionally. Sluggo and I enjoyed walking in it.

Unlike Kassel, the students at Boppard didn't have much contact with the host families because they didn't provide meals. Instead, we got coupons for reduced prices at a number of restaurants. Many of us ate often at the Chinese place because it had the best food in town. Although we were all studying German, it was interesting to note that the various nationalities, including the French, communicated in English when they got together away from school.

Finding the right class was tough. I jumped back and forth several times between two classes because one was too easy and the other too difficult. I never felt I was in the right one.

I was surprised there were no tests, no homework and no final exam. At the *Abschiedsparty* (farewell party), I cornered the administrator and told him I was disappointed the school didn't put more pressure on the students. I was amazed when he said they didn't try hard because they knew no one could learn much in a month. That made *Europa Kolleg* look better than ever.

Fast forward: I later did a story about the Goethe Institute in Berlin which included asking beginning students from around the world why they were taking the course. A husky Brazilian guy said, "So I can read Goethe in the original." I thought, "Good luck, buddy."

For stage three of the *Pause*, Rendelsmann arranged for me to work for six months with Manfred Strastil, the cameraman from Berlin. That started on January 1, 1986, just a few weeks after school finished. Like Mary Beth and Peter, Strastil got a contract to furnish stories to *European Journal* for a certain amount per story. In turn, he gave me a contract. That meant the company got stories from me as usual, but my name never appeared in the books as an employee.

I received the same salary I would have under my *EJ* contract but had a firm quota of 26 stories to do in 26 weeks. Normally, for a variety of reasons, I wouldn't produce quite that many. On rare occasions, I wouldn't have any stories ready. Even when I did have several ready to go, Rex would sometimes say none of them "fit."

I didn't have to move to Berlin. I stayed in the same apartment and went to the office as usual to set up stories, then Strastil, Eva and I would meet somewhere and start shooting. The only major difference from my normal schedule was that I had to edit outside the *Deutsche Welle*.

La catastrophe

Every American over the age of 50 knows where he or she was when President Kennedy was assassinated. The same is true if you mention the *Challenger* explosion to a Baby Boomer.

On January 28, Strastil, Eva and I were traveling through northern France headed for Verdun to do a story on World War One forts that were still standing. It was cold and snowing. On the car radio, I heard the word *catastrophe*. I knew it meant the same thing in English, but I couldn't understand anything else. I asked Eva, who spoke French, what was going on. She told me the space shuttle had exploded. When we got to our hotel in Verdun, the explosion was being rerun over and over on television and color photos were splashed across the front pages of the newspapers.

That was only one of several big stories that broke while we were working together.

On April 15, American planes bombed Libya in retaliation for an explosion in a Berlin nightclub that killed one U.S. serviceman and a Turkish woman. Tensions were high, prompting many Americans to cancel flights across the Atlantic.

As part of a follow-up, I interviewed U.S. tourists in front of the American Express building in Paris, asking if they'd been reluctant to visit Europe because of the possibility of terrorism. They all said no. But I couldn't wait to get away from American Express myself because I thought it would have been a prime target.

Later that month, on April 26, the nuclear reactor at Chernobyl melted down. I heard about it on the radio in a hotel in Luxembourg. We had done some stories there and were preparing to fly to Iceland the next morning. We may have been luckier than most Europeans because we left Luxembourg before the radioactive cloud got there and flew back several days later before it reached Iceland.

Naturally everyone in Europe was nervous about the effects of the meltdown. Electronics shops in West Germany quickly sold out of Geiger counters.

Cars and trucks arriving from the East were checked for radiation and scrubbed down if the readings were too high.

After the meltdown, it rained across most of Western Europe. People were warned not to drink fresh milk or rainwater, and to avoid lettuce and other leafy vegetables. Some playgrounds were closed so children wouldn't be contaminated by fallout washed down by the rain.

I was concerned about Mr. Sluggo who undoubtedly came in contact with wet grass while staying with the Wissemanns during my shoot in Iceland.

Sheep and goats in southern Switzerland got an extra lease on life thanks to Chernobyl. Their slaughter was postponed for several months until radioactive cesium worked its way out of their systems.

There was much confusion about which levels of radiation were safe.

Within three weeks, most of the restrictions had been lifted. Scientists said it was all right to drink fresh milk but they advised waiting a bit longer before eating certain vegetables.

At the outdoor market in Bonn, some vendors had signs saying their lettuce came from greenhouses. But even with drastically reduced prices, there were few buyers.

Rendelsmann asked me to cover the reaction to the meltdown, so I got to speak directly with nuclear experts. They downplayed the danger. Dr. Erich Oberhausen of the Institute for Nuclear Medicine told me West Germany might not have any cancer deaths because of the fallout. He said he would put the number "at between zero and one case in the whole German population."

Scientists insisted a similar disaster couldn't happen in Western Europe, where nuclear facilities generated nearly one-third of the power, because a Chernobyl-type plant wouldn't be able to get a license. But they were concerned about what might happen in the Soviet Union, where the power plants were far less safe and there was no public pressure for change.

Rendelsmann wanted to go all out on the meltdown, so I shot enough material to cut a story running about six minutes. But despite what Peter, Mary Beth and I had suggested earlier regarding variety in the length of packages, Rex wouldn't hear of a story that was double the normal length. He insisted I cut two separate pieces so he could pop up in between to intro part two.

Land of curiosities

I made the first of two visits to Iceland with Strastil. It was a place that interested me, so I dreamed up some stories, got them approved and off we went.

Icelandair paid for our flight and hotel rooms. That would have been forbidden in the United States. Payola, you know. But the people running *European Journal* didn't care. I wouldn't let the freebies influence the way I did my stories anyway. Besides that, if the stories did convince someone to visit Iceland, Icelandair was the only way to get there.

One of the pieces was about the airline itself. I considered it a legitimate story because Icelandair, originally known as Icelandic Air Lines, had revolutionized transatlantic air travel by breaking the price barrier for the first time.

That was in 1953. The government of Luxembourg, which didn't have an airline, asked Icelandic officials if they would fly between New York and Luxembourg. Because Luxembourg charged low landing fees and Icelandic wasn't yet a member of the International Air Transport Association, the airline offered tickets for 30 percent less than existing fares, making transatlantic travel more affordable for the average traveler.

The company president, Sigurdur Helgason, told me, "Our customers, our passengers, they believe in us and we seem to go from generation to generation. Now we see the kids of the hippies. They're on our planes today."

For Icelandair, surviving the price war it started wasn't easy. Britain's Sir Freddie Laker tried cheap fares in 1977 and went broke after five years. Beginning in the 1980s, Virgin Atlantic provided stiffer competition, but both Virgin and Icelandair have managed to co-exist.

When a visitor arrives in Iceland for the first time and makes the half hour ride from Keflavik Airport to Reykjavik, the capitol, he may have the feeling something is missing but can't put his finger on it.

What's missing is trees. The countryside looks like the moon. There are at least two theories on why. One is that the Vikings used all the trees for firewood. Another says sheep ate the bark off the trees, killing them. There were trees in residential areas, but none in the country.

One thing a reporter fears is having a story fall apart, especially when he's a long way from home. It looked as if that was about to happen on a story about NATO, the North Atlantic Treaty Organization.

As we were setting up at the Defense Ministry in Reykjavik, I was running over the questions with an official when he said, "I don't think I'm the right person for this interview."

My heart stopped. Visions of losing the story dashed through my head. We were far from the office in the middle of the North Atlantic. How could I recover?

Fortunately, he picked up the phone, saying, "But I can arrange for you to talk with someone more appropriate."

Whew. What a relief. All we lost was a little time moving to another building.

There's no end to curiosities in Iceland. When Strastil and I were there, there was no television on Thursdays because that was the day off for employees of the TV station.

The phone book listed people by their first names. That's because the father, mother and their male and female offspring all have different last names. And that's because each person's last name is usually based on his or her father's first name. For example, the son of a man whose first name is Jon would have the last name Jonsson. His daughter would be named Jonsdottir, and she would keep that name when she got married.

The duty-free shops at the airport may have been the only ones in the world that were open to both departing and arriving passengers. Icelanders returning home could be seen leaving the building pushing shopping carts brimming with cases of beer. That's because the airport was the only place on the island where full-strength beer was available. Only "near beer" was sold elsewhere – a quirk dating from the days of Icelandic Prohibition. As the story goes, when Prohibition was repealed, the government overlooked beer and the temperance movement raised enough of a protest to keep it banned.

Real beer was finally legalized on March 1, 1989. That date has been celebrated ever since as Beer Day.

We did stories about two Icelandic products, sweaters and skin lotion.

Iceland was renowned for its hand-knit sweaters although they made up less than 10 percent of the total sweater production. Machines did the rest. Hundreds of people, mainly women, knitted the sweaters at home in their spare time. The fastest knitters could produce a sweater in six hours if they worked nonstop. With sheep outnumbering people three to one, there was no shortage of wool.

Icelandair's transatlantic flights always stopped on their home turf, giving travelers access to the duty free shops as well as a chance to buy sweaters. Fortunately for people just passing through, the sweaters didn't cost any more in the airport shops than they did in Reykjavik.

Another natural Icelandic product is a skin lotion that's been shown to be effective against psoriasis and acne. It's made from briny water that bubbles up from deep underground at a place known as the Blue Lagoon, not far from the airport. The lagoon was created by runoff from a geothermal power plant that uses 500 degree subterranean water to produce heat.

The first person to experience the healing effects of the water was a worker from the plant who noticed his psoriasis improved after going for a swim. Since then, many other people have taken a dip in the lagoon and reported good results. A local company started bottling and selling the water.

One day when we were returning to our hotel, my umbrella got crushed in the revolving door. After I threw it away, I noticed I never saw any Icelanders carrying umbrellas, no matter how nasty the weather. I asked about that and was told the locals never use umbrellas because the wind is so strong it destroys them.

Paris

Back on the Continent, we did several stories in Paris. One was about the *International Herald Tribune,* which had been around for nearly 100 years and for Americans was as much a part of the city as the Eiffel Tower and chocolate mousse.

The paper gained worldwide attention in the early 60s when the influential French New Wave film *Breathless* featured Jean Seberg as a *Herald Tribune* street vendor, selling the paper in front of the American Express building.

Since then, the paper has become less European and more global in outlook. By the mid 80s, the *Trib* had expanded to almost all parts of the world and was pushing into the Caribbean. It was printed in five European cities as well as Hong Kong, Singapore and Miami, and the business section was beefed up to better compete with the *Wall Street Journal.*

We roamed through the editorial offices as well as the composing room, where men with thick New York accents who spoke fluent French pasted up the pages and got them ready for printing.

The publisher, Lee Huebner, described a typical reader: "I think of a man I met in Singapore when we first started printing there. He said, 'I grew up in the States, went to college in England and met a woman from France who I later married. We raised our children in France and my family is still there.' But he said, 'I now work for a Saudi Arabian company and they have me on assignment in Southeast Asia, based in Singapore.' And then he happily held up a copy of the *Herald Tribune* and said, 'You know, this is my hometown newspaper.'"

The *Trib* was renamed the *International New York Times* in October, 2013. The *Times* had had sole control of the paper for the previous 10 years.

Another well-known French institution is the *Guide Michelin,* which ranks hotels and restaurants for motorists.

Michelin is a major publisher of maps and other travel materials. In addition to its red guides, which cover hotels and restaurants in many European countries, there are the green guides that describe tourist attractions.

Michelin got into the book business in 1900, just nine years after the Michelin brothers invented the first air-filled tire. There weren't many cars in those days and most people had never been away from home, so Michelin told them where they could eat and sleep as well as where they could get their car repaired when they ventured into new territory.

The red guide has been keeping *restauranteurs* on their toes since 1926 when Michelin started grading them and awarding stars to the best ones.

With hotels and restaurants striving for higher ratings, the books helped raise standards in general. The only drawback was that the recommended businesses became so popular that it was often hard to get in without planning way ahead.

For a story on how hotels and restaurants are graded, Michelin set up an interview with one of the elusive inspectors. The PR people said the only reason they granted the interview was because *European Journal* wasn't broadcast in France. Nevertheless, I couldn't use his name.

The inspector told me he and his colleagues had all attended hotel and restaurant schools and were more secretive than the CIA. They began by visiting a business as a typical guest. Only after the bill was paid did they identify themselves and ask to make a complete inspection. Then they filled out a detailed report used for the annual updating of the guidebook.

The inspectors would move around in a certain area for a year, then switch to a different part of the country. They wouldn't make repeat visits to any area for eight to 10 years.

Restaurants place great importance on the red guide. Once, when the owner of a small Parisian restaurant suffered a heart attack and wound up in the hospital, the first phone call he made was to Michelin, to tell them he wouldn't be acting as chef for a while. Then he called his wife.

Gypsies are the scourge of Paris. They're found wherever tourists hang out, at famous landmarks or shopping areas, because tourists are their prey. Some sit on the sidewalk begging passively, but the pickpockets are aggressive.

For a story on them, Strastil and I spent a few hours at Sacre Coeur, the ornate whitewashed basilica that dominates the Paris skyline.

We watched as three Gypsy women in long, drab peasant dresses and a number of scruffy-looking children hassled tourists entering the church. One woman carried a baby. Another had a blanket wrapped to look as if she had one. As the women approached the tourists with one arm outstretched, the kids tried to pick their pockets, using a folded newspaper or a piece of cardboard to hide their darting hands. The dirty work was left up to the children because French law prohibited the arrest of anyone under the age of 13.

One woman noticed Strastil with his camera and lunged at him, screaming and presumably cursing his unborn children. Unfortunately he wasn't rolling. It would have made a terrific opening shot.

Paris police told us at least 10 people report having their pockets or handbags picked each day during the summer tourist season. Japanese were the favorite targets because they're more polite than other tourists. In a raid on a Gypsy camp, police found about four thousand dollars worth of money in seven different currencies including Singapore dollars.

Most of the gypsies came from the former Yugoslavia. Police said deporting them didn't do much good because they'd soon find their way back to Paris.

The best way for visitors to guard against pickpockets is to keep a good grip on their wallets or handbags when they're in areas frequented by tourists. Or better yet, they can see Paris in the off-season. The Gypsies go south for the winter.

Since I couldn't edit my stories at the *Deutsche Welle,* Strastil had to come up with alternatives. Once, after a week-long shoot, I rode back to Berlin with him and stayed in a hotel for a week writing scripts. He set up a video player and monitor in the room so I could check the tapes. I spent the weekend making shot lists and writing my first story. Monday through Friday I went to a studio each morning to cut a piece, then returned to the hotel to knock out another script. It was grueling, but I was able to fly back to Cologne Friday afternoon, having accomplished five weeks work in almost no time.

On another occasion, Strastil arranged for me to edit at a studio in Meckenheim, not far from Mr. Sluggo's baby-sitters. It was a half hour commute, but staying in my apartment sure beat any hotel room.

Back on the staff

Act II at the *DW*

After my contract with Strastil expired, I returned to the *Deutsche Welle* as planned with a new two-year contract worth 7,000 DM per month. Not only did I get a 1,000 mark raise, but my pay was increasing in dollars because of the shifting exchange rate. It was up to $2,880, an increase of about $150 per week from my starting pay.

At the time, I was the only reporter under contract. Peter and Mary Beth were still supplying stories on their own and there was no shortage of freelancers.

One of them was Deidre Berger, a short, dark-haired woman who worked at North American Radio and often contributed stories to NPR.

Deidre and her visiting sister once rented a car for what turned out to be a disastrous trip to Amsterdam. First, they took a wrong turn and wound up in Luxembourg – quite the opposite direction. After eventually getting to Amsterdam, they went on a shopping spree and left their purchases in the trunk of the car. While the car was parked, someone popped the trunk and took everything.

Another time, Deidre returned from a trip to Ireland saying it was nice to be in a place where her name was so common.

"Berger?" I asked.

"No," she fumed. "Deidre."

Although Diedre did a solid job, some of the newer freelancers who will remain nameless apparently had no broadcasting experience. With Rex editing their scripts, their writing was fine, but their reading left a lot to be desired.

Rex was still producing the show, but Phil Tintner, an American freelancer who lived in Vienna, took over as anchor. It was one of those situations every anchor has nightmares about. Rex went on a three week vacation and Rendelsmann brought in Phil to substitute. But Phil remained in the anchor chair after Rex returned.

Phil was tall and stocky with short blonde hair. He wore Harry Potter glasses long before Harry Potter existed. Everyone liked him because he was a genuine nice guy and a practical joker with a great sense of humor.

Phil often demonstrated his humor with cartoons. After learning we sometimes referred to Rex as Bozo, he drew the clown's face on a sheet of paper, wrote "This is a Bozo-Free Zone" and taped it to the outside of our door. He cleverly added a wart to Bozo's forehead, a wart just like Rex had. Although Rex rarely came to our office, he eventually saw Phil's artwork, but never caught on that it was aimed at him.

Phil had been a very popular morning man at Blue Danube Radio, a government-run English-language station in Vienna. Blue Danube had a weird working schedule: three weeks on and three off. And three weeks meant 21 days straight. The 21-day limit apparently had something to do with getting around a requirement for a work permit.

Phil was one of the few Americans employed at Blue Danube. Most of the disc jockeys or news readers were British radio personalities looking to pick up extra cash during their vacations. Blue Danube paid $1,000 per week.

Phil was eager to improve *European Journal*. With the blessing of Herr Rendelsmann and Prof. Stehr, who turned up in Cologne at least once a year, he convened a meeting of reporters to get everyone's input. Just as Peter, Mary Beth and I had done earlier, he turned out a critique. His major point was that the program desperately needed an American producer "to pull everything together."

At first, Phil commuted between Vienna and Cologne, always traveling by train. He was literally scared to death of flying because he had once been in a commercial plane crash in which some passengers were killed. He would take the night train on Thursdays, arriving in Cologne the next morning. After taping the show in the afternoon, he'd head back to the *Bahnhof.* Eventually Phil got a room in a boarding house a few blocks from the *Deutsche Welle.*

Rendelsmann later hired another American from Blue Danube Radio named Jerry Huffman. Jerry, who had been submitting stories as a freelancer, got a one-year reporter contract which coincided with the last year of my contract.

Jerry was a very likable guy from Wisconsin who looked vaguely like Jay Leno with glasses. He was addicted to Coca-Cola and would arrive at work every morning carrying at least two cans, one of which would be half consumed.

Jerry contended that every writer overused the word "that." After writing his scripts, he'd always go through them carefully to see how many he could remove. I still try to keep <u>that</u> in mind.

The show cycled through several female anchors, but an attractive California girl named Jeannie Hingsen wound up doing it most of the time. Jeannie was shaky at first, but eventually developed a smooth delivery. She was married to Jürgen Hingsen, the German silver medal decathlon winner at the 1984 Los Angeles Summer Olympics. There was speculation that management may have hired her partly because of her name, hoping Olympic fans would tune in.

Another new face

After a few months of anchoring, Tintner wanted out, so Rendelsmann decided to find a replacement other than Rex.

Hoping to avoid the expense of moving someone across the Atlantic, he put an ad in the classified section of the *Herald Tribune.* About a dozen audition tapes came in and Rendelsmann invited the staff to the conference room to watch them. All but one were awful. The exception was submitted by a Canadian named Neil Lundy, and he got the job.

Fortunately Neil had TV experience. He and his wife and two teenaged children were living at a Canadian military base in the German town of Lahr, near Strasbourg, France, where his wife taught school. He had been unemployed.

Neil was tall and thin with dark hair and a complexion so smooth it looked as if he hadn't started shaving. He turned out to be a good, competent anchor, although like many others, he was insecure and always seeking assurance that he was doing a good job.

Return to Iceland

I started off my new contract by covering a few stories in Switzerland: a referendum on nuclear power, an International Red Cross conference in Geneva and a meeting of the International Air Transport Association in Montreux – routine stuff but nevertheless interesting.

Then I worked in another trip to Iceland, and once again Icelandair picked up the tab.

This time I used a local cameraman who, strangely enough, didn't speak a word of English. But his assistant did, so all instructions were relayed through him. Generally, all the younger people in Iceland spoke English. The cameraman, who was in his 30s, somehow slipped through the cracks.

Iceland was at odds with the United States and the International Whaling Commission over how many whales could be killed. Since commercial whaling was outlawed around the world, Iceland, Japan and a few other countries were allowed to harvest the animals for research only.

I made contact with the owner of a whaling ship. We arranged to meet at a dock about half an hour's drive from Reykjavik to get shots of the ship arriving with a minke whale tied alongside. Getting to the ship while it was still at sea had proved to be impossible due to a shortage of time and money.

After the ship was secured, winches hauled the huge creature tail-first up a sloping concrete ramp. Stern-faced men waited, armed with curved cutting tools perched atop long poles. The whale's body was higher than the men were tall and measured about 30 feet long. I was afraid the carving would be gory, but it turned out to be rather clinical as the thick white blubber was stripped away from the red flesh. I felt sorry for the whale which hours earlier had been alive and wild and free.

The ship's owner insisted I have dinner with him that evening. Normally I tried to avoid such things because a typical workday was long and exhausting. But I gave in.

I met him at a Reykjavik restaurant and was surprised when he ordered a whale steak for me. I assumed one purpose of our meeting was to see if I would freak out and reveal myself as an anti-whaling crusader. But I ate it and got away as soon as I could. I was curious about the taste anyway. It was bland.

There had been speculation some whale meat was being fed to mink in order to get rid of it. That provoked a backlash with patriotic Icelanders rushing to buy the meat. Some stores reported a tenfold jump in sales.

Another story was about how President Ronald Reagan and Soviet General-Secretary Mikhail Gorbachev literally put Iceland on the map when they held a summit there in October of 1986. Their meeting took place at Reykjavik's official reception center, Höfði House.

Although the white frame building had been on the waterfront for 80 years, no one showed any interest in it until the summit. After that, it was marked on tourist maps for the first time. The summit also was credited with boosting tourism and creating a bigger demand for Icelandic fish.

We also did a piece about some of Iceland's curiosities. That included getting shots of Swainbjorn Beinteinsson, the bearded high priest of a religion that worshipped Viking gods such as Odinn and Thor. We met him at his simple stone cabin outside Reykjavik where he bowed to a crude statue for the camera.

Mr. Beinteinsson's ancient religion had only about 70 adherents. Nevertheless, it was officially recognized. A young couple learned that the hard way one night when they ran into him after leaving a bar in Reykjavik. Feeling mellow, they asked him to marry them, and he did. They thought it was a great joke until they found out the next morning they really were married.

The last lonely Nazi

Rudolf Hess was the last living link to Hitler's inner circle, one of seven Nazis sent to Berlin's Spandau Prison following the Nuremberg war crimes trial.

Spandau was chosen because it was in West Berlin and the four wartime allied powers – the United States, Britain, France and the Soviet Union – all had easy access to it. The turreted red brick prison was built in the late 19th century and looked like something out of a fairy tale.

Ten high-ranking Nazis were executed after the trial. Marshal Hermann Goering beat the hangman's noose by biting into a cyanide capsule. Hitler confidant Martin Bormann was condemned in absentia. Three others were acquitted.

Of the seven defendants sent to Spandau, four received sentences of either 10 or 20 years. Three others, including Hess, got life. Two of the lifers were released early because of poor health. The Western allies appealed for Hess' release a number of times because of his age, but the Soviets flatly refused. He was a symbol of a time the West wanted to forget and the East wanted to remember.

Although Hess was one of Hitler's chief deputies, he never had any real power. In fact, he may have been trying to boost his standing with the *Fuehrer* when he made a solo flight to Scotland in May of 1941 to try to negotiate a non-aggression pact. The British suspected Hess was crazy. Hitler was certain of it.

After Albert Speer, Hitler's Minister of Armaments, completed his 20-year term in 1966, Hess was the only inmate left in the prison that was built to accommodate 500. Except for a daily one hour walk in the garden, he spent most of his time in a double-sized cell measuring 12 by 20 feet. He had a TV and received four newspapers every day.

Access to Hess was tightly restricted, so it was impossible to get anywhere near him when I went to Berlin to do a story about his confinement.

Working with a Berlin camera crew, we even had to get permission to photograph the outside of the prison, which was set back about 100 yards from the street. In order to get a good angle, the cameraman talked his way into a top floor apartment of a three-story building across the street.

Although we were supposed to remain across the street, we cheated a little and started taking shots from the sidewalk in front of the prison. Almost immediately, the massive two-story-high door opened and a short, white-haired man in a business suit tried to shoo us away. Because of the four-power arrangement, the prison guards were rotated each month. At that time, the Soviets were in charge.

I pretended I didn't understand and walked up to the door. Not surprisingly, the man told me we should move the camera to the other side of the street. Standing behind him were two armed Soviet soldiers, one a giant and the other of normal size, looking like they just stepped out of a James Bond movie. I quickly rejoined the cameraman and we moved across the street to do a standup. We had achieved our objective, getting a shot of the prison showing some activity.

Moments later, three Berlin police cars rolled up, but they couldn't do anything beyond checking our papers because we were in the authorized spot. They suggested we wrap up quickly and move on, which we did.

As part of the story, I interviewed Eugene Bird, a former U.S. military officer who had served as the prison warden for more than 10 years. Bird described Hess as an extreme introvert who was still living in the past, in 1941, thinking what he had done was the right thing for his people.

Hess put an early end to his life sentence by hanging himself on August 17, 1987. He was 93. For the first few days after his death, a group of neo-Nazis held a vigil outside the prison, joined by tourists and curiosity-seekers.

Within two weeks, demolition crews started tearing down the building because the government feared it might become a Nazi shrine. I wondered what might have become of the quaint building if Hess and the other Nazis hadn't been imprisoned there.

Hess was quietly buried in the family plot in the Bavarian town of Wunsiedel. However, his grave eventually became the focus of neo-Nazi rallies, leading his family and cemetery officials to cremate his remains and scatter the ashes in July of 2011.

The more things change ...

To the younger generation, it might seem as if global terrorism began on September 11, 2001 when four hijacked commercial airliners slammed into the World Trade Center in New York City, the Pentagon and a field in Pennsylvania, killing nearly 3,000 people.

But it actually started 31 years earlier when Palestinian hijackers forced three airliners to fly to the Jordanian desert and blew them up – an incident captured on grainy film that was broadcast around the world.

It was September 6, 1970 when the Popular Front for the Liberation of Palestine hijacked four U.S.-bound planes from European airports. Planes belonging to TWA and Swissair were diverted to an old military air strip 30 miles outside the Jordanian capital, Amman.

The other flights were luckier. The crew of an Israeli El-Al plane managed to foil the takeover and the captain of a Pan Am 747 convinced the hijackers to let him land in Cairo, insisting the Jordanian airstrip might not be able to handle such a large aircraft.

But three days later, PFLP sympathizers commandeered yet another plane, a BOAC flight out of Bahrain, and forced it to land in Jordan. (BOAC was British Overseas Airways Corporation. Now it's simply British Airways.)

The more than 400 passengers and crew from the three planes were taken hostage in an effort to force the release of Palestinian militants held in European and Israeli jails. Most of the hostages were freed within six days.

On September 12, the empty aircraft were blown up. The remaining hostages, mostly Jews, were freed by the end of the month. Remarkably, there were no deaths or injuries.

That was not the case two years later when the world was shocked by the murders of 11 Israeli athletes at the Munich Summer Olympics by members of the Palestinian terrorist group Black September.

International terrorism picked up steam during the 1980s, a time when Europe could have been described as a playground for terrorists.

The first major incident of the decade occurred in April 1983 when a bomb went off outside the U.S. Embassy in Beirut, leaving 63 people dead.

In October, a truck bomb destroyed the U.S. Marine Corps barracks at Beirut airport, killing 241 American service personnel. Fifty-eight French paratroopers also died in a nearby bombing, raising the death toll to 299.

In June of 1985, the world was held spellbound as one of the longest lasting hijackings unfolded. The plane was TWA Flight 847, hijacked out of Athens by two Lebanese terrorists who smuggled pistols and grenades through airport security. The aircraft, carrying 153 passengers and crew, went first to Beirut, then made two roundtrips to Algiers in a drama that lasted 17 days.

When the hijackers figured out one of the passengers, Robert Stethem, was a U.S. Navy diver, they beat him, executed him and tossed his body from the plane. The other passengers were gradually released unharmed.

After it was over, the pilot, John Testrake, was hailed for his coolness. The most indelible image of that ordeal was a photo of him looking out the cockpit window as a man behind him brandished a pistol.

Flight attendant Uli Derickson received much praise for keeping the hijackers calm as she encouraged them to release passengers. At one point, she defused a potential crisis by using her own Shell credit card to refuel the plane in Algiers. Cost: $5,000. She also hid the passports of people with Jewish-sounding names.

Sound like a TV movie? It was: *The Taking of Flight 847* **(1988). Lindsay Wagner played Derickson.**
The 1986 film *Delta Force,* **starring Chuck Norris and Lee Marvin, was said to have been inspired by the hijacking.**

A U.S. federal grand jury indicted four men in connection with the hijacking. One was later captured and served 19 years in Germany for Stethem's murder. At this writing, he and two others were on the FBI's Most Wanted Terrorists list. The fourth suspect was reported killed in a car bombing in Syria in 2008.

Numerous other incidents included the hijacking of the Italian cruise ship Achille Lauro in October of 1985. A wheelchair-bound New Yorker named Leon Klinghoffer earned a spot in history when he was killed and his body tossed into the Mediterranean.

In December 1985, simultaneous bombings at check-in counters at the Rome and Vienna airports left 16 dead.

April of 1986 saw the bombing of the LaBelle disco in West Berlin, a nightclub frequented by U.S. servicemen. Two people were killed and scores injured. That was the incident that triggered U.S. air strikes against Libya.

In the same month, a bomb exploded in the passenger compartment of a TWA jet as it approached Athens. Four Americans including a baby were sucked out through a hole in the fuselage but the plane landed safely.

The most horrific terrorist incident of all, of course, was the Pan Am bombing over Lockerbie, Scotland, in December of 1988, which left 270 people dead.

Even before the Pan Am disaster, *European Journal* was doing stories about terrorism and airport security.

We even did a half-hour special on security. I was assigned to the Zurich airport and was privileged to be able to snoop around behind the scenes. Four thousand people worked there. One out of every 10 was a police officer. Some were in uniform, carrying machine guns. Others were in plain clothes, armed with pistols and mingling with the crowds.

One unusual security measure at Zurich was a common check-in area. All passengers reported to the same counter regardless of which airline they were booked on. Such a system may have prevented the carnage in Rome and Vienna, where terrorists targeted people checking in for U.S. and Israeli flights.

Airport officials made sure all workers were wearing proper ID badges. Swissair had been using sky marshals for years.

Germany fights terrorism with an elite commando force called *GSG-9*. The initials stand for *Grenzschutzgruppe-9*, which means Border Protection Group 9.

GSG-9 was formed in 1973, six months after the massacre of Israeli athletes at the Olympics. With memories of the Nazi *SS* still fresh in everyone's mind, Germany had been reluctant to establish any kind of a special military unit. But the ineptitude of the police in dealing with the Black September terrorists in Munich demonstrated the need for one.

To keep *GSG-9* separate from the regular military, the unit is under the control of the Interior Minister and can only be called into action with his approval.

GSG-9's most well-known operation took place in 1977 when commandos followed a hijacked Lufthansa jet to the Somali capital, Mogadishu, and successfully stormed it during the night. Three of the hijackers were killed, a fourth wounded. All 90 passengers and crew were freed without any serious injuries.

Throughout the 80s, *GSG-9* was kept busy matching wits with the Red Army Faction and other homegrown terrorist organizations that included car bombs and remote-controlled explosives in their arsenal.

The commandos spent about 90 percent of their time in training and the rest hunting terrorists.

For a story I put together on the group, *GSG-9* loaned me a video of an actual field exercise. It showed commandos jumping out of a van and abducting a man in broad daylight on a city street. It all happened in seconds. Passersby, who knew nothing about it, watched with their mouths agape.

I did my standup with *GSG-9* paratroopers landing in a field behind me. Tricky but it worked.

Wounded Afghan children might seem to be a relatively new problem, but they've been victims of conflict since Soviet troops rolled into Afghanistan in 1979.

A hospital in Landshut, near Munich, was treating sick and injured Afghan kids during the Soviet occupation, which lasted for 10 years. I met half a dozen boys ranging in age from eight to 14. Two had polio, but the others had either been burned or suffered gunshot wounds. Despite their condition, they were in good spirits and anxious to go home.

The older boys expressed confidence that Afghanistan would succeed in tossing out the Soviets. Ten-year-old Fasal Rabi had been shot in the foot. When asked what he thought about all the Afghans being hurt and killed, he said, "It doesn't matter. It's a fight for independence. We have to suffer."

Those kids would all be more than 30 years old now – if they're still alive.

We gave quite a bit of coverage to AIDS, which surfaced as a big story in Europe as well as the U.S. after Rock Hudson died in 1985.

I did a piece on how the U.S. Army was handling the problem. Before any blood was drawn, the servicemen and women were shown a video dramatizing AIDS cases, a modern version of the classic Army training film.

The first blood tests in Europe showed that for every 1,000 service personnel tested, an average of 1.4 had been exposed to the virus. That was lower than the Army had expected. Those who tested positive were immediately reassigned to the U.S. and stripped of any security clearance. Anyone actually developing AIDS was expected to be granted a medical discharge, meaning he would be eligible for treatment as a veteran.

Even though Iceland was tucked away in the middle of the North Atlantic, it hadn't escaped AIDS.

In doing a story about the disease there, I learned that the island nation had four cases compared with 7,500 in mainland Europe. Of those four, three had died. The lone survivor was a woman who was largely confined to her apartment. The government decided she couldn't be trusted not to spread the disease, so she was constantly chaperoned.

Iceland tried to stay ahead of the problem. The government started an AIDS education program for children as young as 12, two years before the first case was diagnosed on the island.

Blood tests were given to all blood donors as well as most prison inmates, drug users, pregnant women and people reporting to VD clinics.

Strangest interview

France has long had a liberal policy toward political dissidents, welcoming revolutionaries such as Lenin, Ho Chi Minh and the Ayatollah Khoumeini. For a story on how Prime Minister Jacques Chirac was waffling on that policy, I lined up an interview with Abolhassen Bani-Sadr, who was living in France.

Bani-Sadr was Iran's first president following the 1979 Islamic revolution. He was elected in January, 1980, then forced into exile 17 months later because he lacked the support of the fundamentalist parliament.

Bani-Sadr lived in a dilapidated mansion in Versailles. I expected to see a lot of security there because other former Iranian officials had been assassinated, but nothing unusual was apparent at the house.

When the camera crew and I arrived, we were greeted by a man who ushered us through the large front room past a staircase and into a sitting room. The furniture was very basic, nothing fancy. As we set up the equipment, the man kept referring to Bani-Sadr as "the president."

When we were ready, Bani-Sadr came downstairs and sat in an easy chair opposite me. He was a mousy-looking man with large glasses, a full mustache and a receding hairline. There was no one else in sight but I had the feeling his entire entourage was huddled at the top of the stairs listening.

Although Bani-Sadr spoke English, he preferred to answer my questions in French. This put me at a big disadvantage because I had no idea what he was saying. Like a beginning reporter on his first interview, I asked a question, then when he stopped talking, asked another one.

When I returned to Cologne and had the answers translated, I discovered he hadn't responded directly to any of my questions. But I managed to grab an innocuous 17 seconds, so the interview wasn't a total waste.

On another story, the interview went fine but setting it up was strange.

I wanted to do a piece on the 500th anniversary of Britain's College of Arms, a branch of the royal household that grants coats of arms. There was a U.S. tie-in because an exhibit of heraldry was scheduled at the New York Historical Society as part of the celebration.

There were 13 heralds, or genealogists, working at the 300-year-old headquarters building in London. All had unusual titles. For my interview, I was directed to Patric Dickenson, whose title was *Rouge Dragon,* French for red dragon. (In proper French, it's *Dragon Rouge.*)

I dialed his number and asked to speak with Mr. Dickenson. Click! Someone hung up.

Maybe I had a wrong number. I tried again. Click!

Then – I don't know how I thought of it – but I called back and asked to speak with the *Rouge Dragon.*

"Speaking."

After that, everything went smoothly.

In London, we photographed some of the 11,000 books, manuscripts and other records used to trace bloodlines as far back as the 8th century, and I came face-to-face with the *Rouge Dragon,* a slight, well-dressed young man. He told me the College of Arms was the only place in the world where people with British names could be sure of getting an authentic coat of arms. If one didn't exist, he said the college could design it for about $1,200.

He noted, however, that nine out of 10 Americans who think they're related to British aristocracy are not.

I never did ask the *Rouge Dragon* why he didn't answer to his real name.

I always tried to keep my interviews at a reasonable length, although I seldom succeeded, because I transcribed them to help in plotting the story. The shorter the interview, the less I had to type.

In the Alsace region of northeast France, I did a story

about an outdoor museum in Ensisheim where old houses were being reassembled after having been hauled in from the countryside. The goal of the project was to preserve the area's cultural heritage. At least 20 homes had been rebuilt, the newest being at least 170 years old.

For the sound bite, I spoke with the man in charge of the project. Since it was a simple story and I already had plenty of background, I wrapped up the interview after about five minutes, saying, "That's it. Thank you."

He gave me a startled look and asked, "That's all? That's all?"

I didn't want to disappoint him, so I thought up a few more questions. He obviously wasn't aware that he'd be lucky to get 15 seconds on the air. As it turned out, I didn't use any of the interview.

Tapestry

The 16th and 17th centuries were the golden age for tapestries in Europe, a time when kings commissioned them as symbols of power, used them as room dividers and sometimes took them along while traveling to provide a touch of home.

I learned there was at least one place left in Europe where it was possible to get a tapestry repaired or have a new one made from scratch – the Gaspar de Wit factory in the Belgian city of Mechelen, located halfway between Brussels and Antwerp.

Gaspar de Wit might better be described as a studio than a factory. Appropriately, the business was housed inside a restored 15th century abbey. When I visited to shoot a story, most of the 20 employees were working at looms in a large room with a very high ceiling.

Spools of yarn were kept in cubbyholes along one wall, cubbyholes that looked like mail slots behind the reception desk of a big hotel. The spools were arranged chromatically so that red gradually changed to orange, then yellow, then green, then blue. Natural light streaming in through large windows made the colors vibrant.

Using old techniques on old equipment, some women were restoring tapestries from museums in Japan and France. Others were creating new designs, some of them abstracts. One woman was working from a photograph, recreating a tapestry that was destroyed by fire in a German castle.

An easy renovation could take several months. Weaving a new piece might take a couple of years, depending on the size and design. The work progressed at a rate of about one square meter per month and the price ranged from three to six thousand dollars for each square meter.

Three degrees of separation

According to the theory "six degrees of separation," anyone in the world is just six persons removed from anyone else. A game involving the actor Kevin Bacon is used to demonstrate that he can be linked with any other actor.

Putting this theory to practice, I discovered to my amazement that I was only three degrees away from Vincent van Gogh. That's because I interviewed a man in the Netherlands who had spoken with an old man who had known van Gogh as a child. The old man said he thought Vincent was crazy because he asked him to climb trees and fetch bird's nests so he could sketch them.

The man I interviewed operated a small van Gogh museum in the southern town of Nuenen, near Eindhoven. Vincent had lived there with his parents from 1883 to 1885 and it was there that he painted *The Potato Eaters*. The van Gogh home was still standing, right on the main street, but was occupied and not open to the public.

I did that interview in connection with a rare exhibition of van Gogh's sketches at the Kroller-Muller museum, located in a national park not far from Arnhem.

I noticed van Gogh didn't sign all his paintings and

wondered why. When I asked the museum director, he said Vincent only put his name on paintings he liked.

He sold only one painting during his life. I asked the director what Vincent's reaction might be if he could come back and see his paintings were selling for millions of dollars. He told me, "Oh, he'd probably say, 'I knew it would happen. I just didn't know how long it would take.'"

I visited other locations associated with van Gogh while roaming around Europe, including the asylum at St. Remy in Provence, where he had committed himself from May 1889 to May 1890. He did a great deal of work in that year, notably many paintings dominated by a giant sun.

I had a British travel guide that said it was possible to see his room, but nothing could have been further from the truth. The asylum had been in use continuously for centuries and there was a sign at the main entrance stating in several languages that you shouldn't even think of entering unless you had business there.

I later read a newspaper article by a writer who was confronted by the same sign. He claimed he had climbed up a rain gutter on the old stone building and found Vincent's room before he was thrown out. He said he identified the room by matching the view from the window with some of van Gogh's paintings.

The asylum didn't forget its most famous patient. There was a bust of him in the garden.

On another trip, I visited Auvers-sur-Oise, a small town near Pontoise, northwest of Paris, where van Gogh lived the last two months of his life. He rented an attic room in an inn called the Auberge Ravoux, which is on the main street. Vincent's room wasn't open to the public at that time, but the entire building was restored and reopened in 1992.

After asking directions half a dozen times in broken French, I found the little cemetery where he's buried. It was on a bluff above the town, surrounded by a wheat field. Next to Vincent is the grave of his brother Theo, who died six months later. Theo was originally buried in the Netherlands, but his wife felt that since the brothers had been very close in life, they should be together in death, so she had his body moved to Auvers.

Vincent died on July 29, 1890, two days after suffering a gunshot wound to the chest. Until recently, it was believed the wound had been self-inflicted. But in a book entitled *Van Gogh: The Life*, published in October 2011, authors Steven Naifeh and Gregory White Smith said their research showed he'd actually been shot accidentally by two teenaged boys. Vincent, on his deathbed, had refused to implicate anyone.

Jacques Brel lives on

I decided to do a piece on the Belgian singer-composer Jacques Brel because his albums were selling better after his death than when he was alive. Brel was brought to the attention of American audiences in the mid-70s through the English language revue, *Jacques Brel is Alive and Well and Living in Paris*. His songs were also translated into many other languages including Swedish and Polish.

For the story, I interviewed one of his three daughters, France, who ran the Brel Foundation in Brussels. The foundation's expansive office resembled a museum. I never quite figured out what its purpose was other than to promote Mr. Brel.

France Brel had that freshly scrubbed look of someone loaded with money. She was well-dressed and very attractive with her black hair in a page boy cut. She told me she believed her father's songs had endured because he sang of universal feelings.

Another person interviewed for the story, biographer Olivier Todd, noted that Brel did curtain calls but never an encore. He reasoned that actors don't come out and recite more lines, so why should he sing another song?

Brel took an interest in French Polynesia later in life, staying on the island of Hiva Oa in the Marquesas, where van Gogh's friend, fellow artist Paul Gauguin had lived. Brel died of lung cancer in Paris in 1978 at the age of 48. His body was returned to Hiva Oa and buried just a few yards from Gauguin.

Sherlock Holmes

Fans of Sherlock Holmes who set out to see what's at 221B Baker Street in London may be surprised to find new apartments behind an old façade.

Technically, there is no such address. Never was. The apartments have a string of numbers encompassing 221.

For most of the past century, that site was the headquarters of a bank called Abbey National. Soon after it opened in 1932, letters addressed to Sherlock Holmes started arriving from all over the world at an average of one each day. Not wanting to disappoint Holmes' admirers, the bank designated a secretary to send out replies purportedly signed by the legendary detective.

That continued until 2002 when Abbey National relocated and the interior was rebuilt as apartments.

Aware of the worldwide interest in Holmes, I made it a point to cover a pilgrimage by the Sherlock Holmes Society to the town of Meiringen in central Switzerland.

Meiringen was idyllic, a remarkably clean place with plenty of classic Swiss chalets surrounded by snow-capped mountains. The town marked one of the high points in Holmes' career because it was there that he battled his archenemy Professor Moriarty at the nearby Reichenbach Falls.

I traveled there with a freelance Swiss camera crew. The photographer picked me up at Zurich airport, then we drove through the Alps to Meiringen and stayed overnight in a hotel.

The next morning, 81 members of the Sherlock Holmes Society dressed in Victorian costumes gathered at the base of a funicular railway and rode to the top of the 300-foot-tall waterfall. They came from nearly a dozen countries. Most were British, but the United States, Australia and Japan were well represented. It was chaotic because the participants seemed to be outnumbered by a swarm of reporters and photographers who included a large number of Japanese.

At a viewing area close enough to the falls to be covered by a fine spray, two society members dressed as Holmes and Moriarity staged a fistfight. My photographer didn't seem to grasp what was going on, even though all the other cameras were pressing in on the action. I had the feeling he normally worked weddings. I waved to get his attention and pointed to the two men scuffling, but I couldn't tell if he got any of it on tape.

The battle ended when Holmes and Moriarity ducked aside and society members hurled two mannequins off the cliff.

The guest of honor was Jean Conan Doyle, daughter of Holmes' creator, Sir Arthur Conan Doyle. She was a petite white-haired woman who seemed somewhat frail. Reporters had been warned at a briefing beforehand that interviews with her were forbidden. Although I normally wasn't very competitive because I didn't have to be, I couldn't resist. When she came near, I stuck the microphone in her face and asked, "What do you make of all this?"

Dame Jean graciously stopped and said it was all very exciting. Nothing earthshaking, but I felt it would add interest to the piece, and it did.

Back in Cologne, I discovered I had the interview but the photographer had completely missed the tossing of the mannequins. One of the German networks had been there, so I ordered a copy of their tape to fill the gap. I suggested to the woman in charge of hiring freelance photographers that she never use that guy again.

There's a little museum on Baker Street that claims to be the "real" 221B. However, members of the Sherlock Holmes Society point out that the actual address of the museum is number 239.

Go West

Germans have a special affinity for the American Wild West thanks to a 19th Century writer named Karl May.

I had never heard of Karl May until I started living in Germany. That was one of the first things many Germans would ask: Did I know of him? When I said no, they were happy to fill me in.

Long before he ever set foot in the United States, May (pronounced "my") entertained millions with the adventures of Old Shatterhand and his Indian companion Winnetou, an Apache warrior. Shatterhand was a German civil engineer who roamed the American frontier. He was so-named because he could pulverize a man's face with one punch.

May, who lived from 1842 to 1912, was said to have been inspired by James Fenimore Cooper's *The Last of the Mohicans*. Although he published his first Wild West book in 1875 and wrote the last one before 1900, he didn't visit the United States until 1908. He authored more than 60 books, but not all were Westerns. His publisher claims to have printed 100-million copies over the years.

Even today, Germans continue buying May's books, although interest has waned among the younger generation since the advent of computers and video games.

Eleven Winnetou films were made during the 60s, and they're still being recycled on German TV. The American actor Lex Barker, remembered for playing Tarzan in the early 1950s, often portrayed Old Shatterhand.

A Temporary European

Thousands gather at pow-wows staged around Germany to play cowboys and Indians. The biggest one is the annual festival at Bad Segeberg, north of Hamburg, where as many as a quarter of a million people have turned out during the summer to watch a swashbuckling theatrical production based on episodes from May's books.

Some Winnetou fans travel to the United States to look for the real thing. Among them was Christine Beyert, a vivacious blonde who worked as a research assistant at the *Deutsche Welle*. On one of her vacations, she met up with her friend Rosy, a massage therapist living in Los Angeles who also happened to be a good-looking German blonde. They rented a VW van and headed to the Southwest to find Indians. After learning of a celebration at one reservation, they drove there.

As Christine told it, an Indian man stopped them, saying, "Sorry, no white folks allowed."

"But we're German!" the girls chanted in unison.

"Oh, OK. C'mon in."

It's hard to believe any Indians would practice such discrimination but the story has a cute punchline.

One thing leads to another

The toughest part of the job was coming up with new projects. Peter, Mary Beth and I would often be working on at least half a dozen stories in various stages of development. But occasionally we'd get caught up and have to start scrounging for ideas. Miraculously, after a dry spell, we always managed to find something.

On rare occasions, one story would lead to another. Once, Rendelsmann assigned me a piece about a little museum in the Hürtgen Forest, an area near Aachen which saw heavy fighting during World War Two. The fighting was so intense and so many officers were lost that Ernest Hemingway suggested in his novel *Across the River and Into the Trees* that it would have been better for the GIs to shoot the new battalion commanders as they got off the trucks so their bodies wouldn't have to be retrieved later. It took the U.S. Army nearly four months, with the loss of 33,000 lives, to advance only six and a half miles.

One thing I learned from doing that story was that the bodies of both U.S. and German troops were still being found, and parts of the country were littered with unexploded bombs, grenades and other ordnance. And that was four decades after the war.

Whenever land had to be cleared for a highway, new homes or any other kind of construction, especially in heavily bombed parts of Germany such as Cologne and Hamburg, workers would sweep the area with metal detectors and carefully check out anything suspicious.

I produced a fresh story on that angle that turned out to be more interesting than the original piece. I personally saw rusty land mines being dug up as well as 50 caliber machine gun bullets found in perfect condition. The bullets were packed in grease inside a metal box and it looked as if they could have been fed into a gun and fired immediately.

Another story looked at American expatriates in Europe. It featured a man who was a successful artist in Paris, a woman who sold jewelry in Brussels and a writer who helped support himself with acting roles in movies shot in Berlin. The writer was a black American. That gave me the idea to do a piece on why black Americans live in Europe. It turned out to be my most meaningful story.

When I proposed the idea to Rendelsmann, he immediately rejected it, saying the topic was "too hot for American television." I mentioned that to a black American woman who occasionally freelanced as a reporter and she thought it was a terrific idea. She convinced Rendelsmann to reverse his decision.

Featured in the story was Donald Jones, one of the most fascinating people I've ever met. Jones was an actor, dancer and all-around entertainer living in Amsterdam. He spoke Dutch fluently and was so well known that he could walk down the street in any town in the Netherlands and virtually everyone would recognize him.

Jones was originally from Harlem. He went to Europe as a member of a song and dance troupe that became stranded in Italy when the manager ran off. Most of the dancers made their way back to the United States, but Jones and a few others decided to stay in Europe.

The best way to tell the story is to resurrect the script:

>NARRATION: A St. Louis showgirl named Josephine Baker is one of the best-known black Americans to have lived in Europe. She was the toast of Paris in the 1920s, an era when black Americans started migrating to the Continent.
>Another American who spent much of his life in Paris was Sydney Bechet, a major figure in the New Orleans school of jazz.
>
>STANDUP: No one knows how many black Americans came to Europe over the years or how many live here now. But it's generally acknowledged that one thing that draws them here is less discrimination.
>
>NARRATION: Donald Jones is a celebrity in Holland. On this night, he's co-starring in the Dutch version of the play *I'm Not Rappaport*, in a town near Amsterdam. Jones came to Europe more than 30 years ago with a song and dance group and he's been here ever since.
>
>QUESTION: Is facing discrimination in the States part of the reason you stayed here and didn't go back there?

JONES: Yes, because I lived here, *I lived,* I lived here. You could go anywhere you wanted to go, you could eat anywhere, you could go in any hotel and there was not that stopgap feeling – can I go into that hotel? That disappeared slowly but surely, and I like that feeling. When I'm in the States, especially down South, there's a kind of politeness these times. But that politeness still gives way to a feeling that discrimination has not completely disappeared in America. It's just been subdued.

NARRATION: Paris is a part time home for Patricia French, the director of Gazelle International, a new cosmetics company catering to dark-skinned women. Originally from Georgia, she now lives in both the U.S. and France.

FRENCH: I started a company here in France and I succeeded in building something and making headway for myself, which would not have been available to me in the U.S. In this case, being black was last, whereas being black in the U.S. and starting a cosmetics company would have been my first negative.

NARRATION: Joseph Billups retired from the U.S. Army in Germany. He now works for a pesticide company, training third world countries in the use of the product.

BILLUPS: I personally feel that racial problems exist throughout the world. It's how a person conducts himself. Of course there are prejudices against certain people. For instance in Europe I find that there's no more prejudice against the blacks than there are against people like the Turks.

A Temporary European

NARRATION: Blacks from Africa, the Caribbean and the United States feel a kinship because of their color, but they are separated by their culture.

FRENCH: I spend quite a bit of time, at least three or four days a month in Africa, in West Africa. How do they view American blacks? They view American blacks as being more white than black. They don't really relate to us as being Africans.

BILLUPS: See, I get in conversations with the Africans. I say, "Well, you know you're lucky because you know your roots. I don't." They say, "Yeah, but you're lucky because you're American. Roots don't mean anything."

JONES: You should know who your ancestors are. We don't know that, and that's the biggest disadvantage we American blacks have. We don't know who the hell our forefathers were, which village we came from. I'd like to know. I'd love to know. But I'll never know.

NARRATION: Donald Jones is just one of the black Americans who most likely will never move back to the United States. But even though some may feel bitter about discrimination in their own country, they still say they're glad to be American.

The story took a year to shoot because I couldn't just zip from one location to another to do the interviews. I had to wait until I had another reason to be in Frankfurt, Paris or Amsterdam.

When I set up the interview with Billups, I told him I wanted to talk about the differences in discrimination between the United States and Europe. He asked, "Do you want the truth?"

I said, "Yes, absolutely."

But when I arrived with a camera crew, his comments became fairly lame. I'm still wondering what "the truth" was, and whether it was the German crew or the camera that muzzled him.

It wasn't unusual for someone to be talkative on the phone, then clam up when the camera started rolling.

A good example was Charles Masy, a portly, grizzled bar owner in Brussels who was reputed to be a recruiter of mercenaries. Masy claimed to have been a mercenary himself once, serving in the Congo and Yemen. His bar, the Renaissance, was located just a couple of blocks from the Grand Place in the center of the city. It was a hangout for both veteran and would-be mercenaries. A bunch of tough-looking guys lined the bar, many wearing black leather jackets with Vietnam designs on the back.

Masy had spoken freely about the recruiting business when I phoned him, but when it came time for the formal interview he became very hesitant, reminding me that recruiting mercenaries was against the law.

It was difficult to find a usable sound bite, but I managed to grab a short quote and finish the story anyway. Luckily I was able to fill it out with good video from German TV of mercenaries training in Alabama. The story was topical because investigators in Stuttgart had recently seized a large quantity of weapons and arrested three men on charges of trying to organize a team of mercenaries to fight in the Middle East.

Cyprus

As far as I knew, *European Journal* hadn't done any stories about Cyprus, the island off the Turkish coast in the eastern Mediterranean. I thought it would be fun to go there, so I conjured up some ideas and got them approved.

I had a feeling I might run into problems because two days before I was scheduled to leave, a hijacked Kuwaiti airliner landed at Larnaca airport and was still there. But since I had four stories set up, I decided to go anyway and see what would happen. I had hired a local cameraman through the *Deutsche Welle* and was traveling alone.

Although Larnaca served as the international airport for Cyprus, it was small by international standards. Most of the people flying in were European tourists on their way to nearby beach resorts. The terminal was so small that the planes parked a short distance away and passengers exited using stairways on wheels.

When I got there, the hijacked Kuwaiti 747 with more than 100 people on board was sitting some distance away on the tarmac shimmering in the afternoon sun. More than a dozen cameras were set up on the roof of the terminal, all pointing at the jet. The photographers lounged nearby. Earlier, the hijackers had killed a passenger and dumped his body onto the tarmac. Many of the cameras were rolling nonstop so they wouldn't miss anything. With videotape, they could record over and over.

Inside, in a second floor office, a crowd of reporters was gathered around a transistor radio placed in the middle of a table, trying to pick up conversations between the hijackers and the tower. I was glad I wasn't one of them.

I discovered my cameraman was among those on the roof. But he was no longer *my* cameraman. He explained he had a contract with ITN in London to cover any stories they wanted and couldn't leave the airport as long as the hijacked plane was there. So my first job was to find another cameraman who could start shooting the next morning.

I considered doing a standup with the Kuwaiti plane in the background so I could put together a generic hijacking story later. The former cameraman even offered to shoot it, but I couldn't instantly plot a story in my head. Besides, the way things go, I knew there was a chance something dramatic might happen when the camera was on me and he'd miss it.

Getting to my hotel wasn't easy. The airport was on the southeast coast and the hotel was in Nicosia, the capital, which was in the middle of the island. It was nearly a one hour drive and I had to travel by bus to hold down expenses. But despite being a savvy traveler, I got taken for a ride, literally.

I questioned a number of airport employees and they all insisted there was no bus to Nicosia, I'd have to go by taxi. So I did. I found out later the trick was to take a taxi to Larnaca, nine miles away, then catch a bus. But no one at the airport would clue me in. A great conspiracy.

I knew the folks in the *Deutsche Welle* travel office would get excited when I submitted an astronomical taxi bill, and they did. But I got reimbursed anyway.

Once at the hotel, I phoned the local TV station and talked with the news director. I was in luck. He referred me to a freelance photographer. I called him and he agreed to shoot for me. He said he was the only photographer on the island who wanted nothing to do with the hijacking.

The main story we did was about the standoff between the Greek and Turkish Cypriots. Cyprus was a Mediterranean version of Germany, divided by a wall that separated the Turkish Cypriots in the north from the Greek Cypriots in the south. The wall ran right through Nicosia, something like the situation in Berlin.

Hostilities had begun soon after Cyprus gained independence from Britain in 1960. The separation became complete in 1974 when Turkish troops moved into the northern third of the island in response to a Greek-backed coup. Turkey was the only government in the world to recognize the Turkish Cypriot state.

I didn't realize the Greek and Turkish Cypriots had originally lived side-by-side in communities all over the island. Only after 1974 did the two groups concentrate in the north and south, often literally trading homes.

One of the people I interviewed was George Vassiliou, the president. What amazed me was the apparent lack of security at the presidential palace. Despite the tensions on the island, we drove right up and walked in the front door without anyone questioning us.

Because of its close proximity to the Middle East, violence occasionally spilled over into Cyprus in the form of bombings and assassinations. Cyprus had a liberal immigration policy and it depended heavily on tourism, so it was easy for agents and *provocateurs* to slip in.

President Vassiliou said his government was dealing with the problem on two levels. First, trying to convince other countries in the area to leave Cyprus out of their quarrels. Secondly, having a good police force to keep an eye on everything.

Cyprus was also a smuggling center. The harbormaster at Limassol told me some ships coming out of Middle Eastern ports would change their name at sea so it would be more difficult to track them. He said a ship once arrived with its name painted on the bow upside down.

Another story we shot focused on Middle East Airlines, or MEA, one of the great survivors of the airline business. Privately-owned MEA was based in Lebanon. During that country's long civil war, Beirut airport was often shut down due to shelling, once for as long as four months.

MEA continued flying between Europe, the Middle East and Africa. But since planes on the ground in Beirut were uninsurable, the airline's home base became primarily a transit point. MEA used a variety of means to stay in business including closing offices, hauling freight and leasing some of its planes to other airlines.

An MEA vice president flew in from Beirut to do an interview for the story. When we met for dinner the night before, he suggested the cameraman and I might want to fly to Beirut – just a short hop away – to get shots at the airport. It was a scary thought since Westerners were still being kidnapped in Lebanon, but I wanted to see how far it would go. Luckily he dropped the idea.

The Kuwaiti plane left while I was still in Cyprus. The hijacking ended peacefully in Algiers.

With all the flying I did, there were very few problems. The only time anything unusual happened was when KLM lost my suitcase after a flight from San Francisco to Amsterdam.

I went to the lost luggage counter and told the woman my suitcase hadn't turned up. She said, "I know. We have a new baggage sorting system and it doesn't work."

I flew on to Cologne. The suitcase was to be delivered to my apartment later that evening. Knowing the bag was coming, I tried to stay awake but couldn't fight the urge to doze off. The doorbell woke me and I raced to the door. I was so bewildered from jet lag that I couldn't figure out why the man holding my suitcase was speaking German.

I once flew to Munich to do a piece on whether a favorable exchange rate was attracting more American tourists. A freelance camera crew picked me up at the airport and we drove into the city. Our first stop was the American Express office, where I was going to interview an executive.

Before going in, I ducked into a washroom to check my appearance only to find the collar of my white shirt stained with blood. I had put in a new razor blade that morning and my collar had a streak of blood along the neck several inches long. I loosened my tie and washed the collar with the liquid soap provided. It was wrinkled the rest of the day, of course, but I got by, even did a standup.

I was baffled by the fact that no one had said anything – not the check-in people at the airport, not the flight attendants, not even the camera crew.

The funniest thing I ever saw at an airport: I was standing around with a camera crew outside a small office building at the Düsseldorf airport waiting to interview someone inside. Over the public address system, there was an announcement asking the owner of an Opel parked in front of the building, license plate such-and-such, to report to his car.

Everyone in the immediate area, at least half a dozen people, turned to look at the car. Inside was a large dog, something like a Great Dane, sitting on the front passenger seat gnawing chunks out of the padded dashboard.

Moments later, the apparent owner of the car – a woman – came running up. When she saw what was happening, she stopped in her tracks, put her hands to her face and screamed.

The beloved 2CV

I convinced Rendelsmann to let me do a story about the strange little French car called the 2CV. Spelled out, that's *Deux Chevaux*, which means two horses.

The car actually had nine horsepower when it came into being in 1949, but it was listed as two horses for tax purposes. Later models were a friskier 29 HP.

Like the Volkswagon Beetle, Citroën's 2CV was turtle-shaped but a little longer. It was said to be so basic that almost anyone could take it apart and fix it. The engine sounded like a sewing machine. The headlights poked up like periscopes from the fenders.

Unlike ordinary cars, the side windows didn't roll down; they were hinged in the middle horizontally and could be held open with clips. Like my Renault truck, the gearshift stuck out of the dashboard.

The 2CV was intended as a basic car for use in rural France. In fact, one of the tests it had to pass was rolling across a plowed field carrying a basket of eggs without breaking any. But despite its humble beginnings, the 2CV quickly reached cult status with the general public.

For anyone who was unaware of the 2CV, the car gained international attention in 1981 when Roger Moore drove one during a chase scene in the James Bond film, *For Your Eyes Only*. That prompted a big fad among 2CV owners in Germany – putting decals on their cars that looked like bullet holes.

The news peg for my story was a rumor that the 2CV's days were numbered. I learned that was true. Sales had been sagging, especially in France. What sealed the car's fate was the imposition of tighter air pollution laws in Switzerland and Austria that effectively banned further imports. Those two countries had accounted for up to 20% of sales.

When word of the 2CV's impending demise got out, sales soared in Germany where it was affectionately known as *Die Ente,* or the duck, short for ugly duckling.

The last 2CVs rolled off the assembly line at a factory in Portugal in July, 1990. Over the years, Citroën made more than five million of them. The last ones sold for a base price of about $5,000.

There were some 200 2CV clubs in Europe, more than half of them in Germany. Dozens of 2CV get-togethers were held across the Continent every summer, often several at the same time in different countries.

I went with a *Hausteam* to the Rhine Valley town of St. Goarshausen to cover one of the gatherings. Owners of 2CVs and other Citroën models strolled around checking out each other's vehicles, many of which were outrageously customized. One 2CV was mounted on top of a large Citroën van, forming an improvised camper. Grafted Mercedes grills were popular. There were duck decorations everywhere, including rubber ducks used as hood ornaments.

The camaraderie went beyond the rallies. We later shot a wedding elsewhere in Germany where everyone in attendance drove a 2CV. When the bride and groom left the church, they walked under a canopy of 2CV hoods held aloft in their honor. At the reception, one of the gifts was a chess set and the chess pieces were ducks.

Even though the 2CV hasn't been made for more than two decades, fan clubs still exist in Europe. Not surprisingly, there are also 2CV web sites.

Four-legged friends

People on both sides of the Atlantic always asked if my dog had to stay in quarantine when he arrived in Germany. The answer was no. Quarantines have been used primarily on islands such as Great Britain and Hawaii. There never was a quarantine in Germany. The main problem there, as well as in Central Europe, was infected foxes.

As of January 2012, Britain waived quarantine requirements for dogs and cats entering from the European Union as well as countries including the United States, Canada and Australia providing they were microchipped, vaccinated against rabies and treated for tapeworm (dogs only). But in the 80s, all dogs and cats, no matter where they came from, had to spend six months in quarantine. No exceptions. And it wasn't cheap. A typical stay in a kennel cost about $1,200 for a dog and $900 for a cat.

Being a dog lover, I was curious about the effects of the British quarantine on our four-legged friends, so I did a story on it. The aim of the confinement, of course, was to keep rabies out of the UK. Officials at the Ministry of Agriculture claimed some pets had actually died of the disease while in quarantine.

At the time I did my story, about 4,500 dogs were quarantined and 75 of them had died in a one year period. The government insisted loneliness was never a factor – that most pets died from sickness or old age – but that was a hard sell for people who believed their quarantined pets had succumbed to broken hearts.

In Germany, whenever there's a sign at the edge of a forest that says *Tollwut* (rabies), it means there's been at least one case of rabies in the area. And experts believe that for every case they know of, at least 30 animals are infected.
Since rabies was spread mainly by wild foxes, the German government was experimenting with a plan to vaccinate as many as possible. Veterinarians couldn't bring the foxes in for shots, so they took the vaccine to them, hidden inside chicken heads or blocks of fishmeal shaped like tiny hockey pucks.
Workers would fan out through the forest and place the bait along likely fox runs. The vaccine was packed under pressure in plastic capsules so when the fox bit into the bait it would spray into his mouth. Researchers could tell how effective the vaccination was by studying the discarded capsules.
Since we didn't have unlimited time like the *National Geographic,* we got shots of workers dispersing chicken heads, but we couldn't wait for the foxes to show up.

One advantage for dogs living in Europe was the fact that there wasn't any heartworm, an often-fatal affliction spread by mosquitoes that's found all over the United States. No heartworm meant dog owners didn't have to buy and administer the monthly preventatives.

We're all familiar with the classic image of a Swiss rescue dog – a St. Bernard with a miniature barrel of whisky attached to his collar. I wondered what the truth was. The best way to find out was to do a story.
Working with a group of volunteers in Geneva, I learned that St. Bernards actually had been used as rescue dogs until the mid-60s. But due to their huge size and weight,

they were phased out as helicopters took on a larger role in rescues.

The new rescue dogs came in all shapes and sizes although most were German Shepherds. They worked all kinds of disasters all around the world. One job the Swiss dogs had taken part in was searching for survivors following an earthquake in Mexico City.

At dawn on a frosty Sunday morning, the dogs and their owners gathered in a forest outside Geneva for one of their periodic practice sessions. It was winter and there were more leaves on the ground than in the trees. The volunteers, about a dozen of them, lined up along a dirt road with their dogs, standing about 50 feet apart. When everyone was ready, they released the dogs and started walking slowly though the trees. Each dog swept back and forth, turning on command, covering every inch like a long row of windshield wipers.

Before they started, a man portraying the victim walked a few hundred yards into the forest and lay down in a slight indentation.

Each dog had to remain silent until the man was found. After about 10 minutes, one of them started barking. The victim had been found. The lucky dog was a Sheltie.

In the German-speaking world, a German Shepherd is known as a *Schäferhund,* which translates literally as shepherd's dog.

Travels with Mr. Sluggo

Although Mr. Sluggo might have been interested in taking part in the training exercise, he was stuck at home.

He did get around Europe quite a bit though, riding in the back of the truck whenever I went exploring. He didn't seem to care much for the truck. Although there was plenty of room in the back, which was carpeted so he wouldn't slip and slide, the window in the rear door was far above his eye level.

Sluggo traveled as far north as Århus in Denmark. That was a trip to Legoland, which featured scale models of well-known landmarks such as Mt. Rushmore made entirely of Lego bricks. It struck me as more of a place for kids than adults. When we crossed into Denmark from Germany and I flashed my U.S. passport, the border guard seemed genuinely thrilled to see me. Apparently not many Americans traveled that road.

The eastern extreme for Mr. Sluggo was Auschwitz in southern Poland. He and I tagged along with a longtime friend, Jim Warras of Los Angeles, who had rented a car.

In order to reach Poland, we had to drive through Czechoslovakia, and we needed a doggie health certificate that we picked up during a brief stay in Vienna. To get the certificate, we had to drive around Vienna looking for the *Amt Tierarzt,* the official vet's office. While Jim and Sluggo waited in the car, I went into the office, which was inside a huge prewar apartment building. For a few schillings, the vet filled out a form stating he had examined the dog and found him to be in good health, even though Sluggo never left the car.

Everything went smoothly until we got to the Polish border and the customs man pointed out that Poland was not mentioned on the health certificate. I had asked the vet to list both Czechoslovakia and Poland, but I made the mistake of sticking the certificate in my pocket without looking at it.

I was sent to a back room in the customs building where the grubbiest looking government official I had ever seen sat behind a desk. He was slightly rotund, badly in need of a shave and dressed in a rumpled plaid shirt.

Using a combination of basic English and German, he pointed out that the dog was not authorized to enter Poland because Poland was not listed on the certificate. I said if the dog was healthy in Czechoslovakia, just a few meters away, it stood to reason he would also be healthy in Poland. He grinned, revealing a few missing teeth, then offered to amend the certificate for a small fee.

It was clear we were playing a game. I said I'd have to get money out of the car, so I ran outside. I had no intention of giving him paper money of any kind, so I gathered some coins and returned. I made little stacks on the edge of the desk with coins from Czechoslovakia, Austria and Germany, saying that was all the money I had. It added up to less than one dollar. He surprised me by scooping up the coins without comment. He scribbled something on the certificate and off we went.

I found Auschwitz to be a very sad place but almost too neat and kind of sterile. Some of the two-story barracks had displays inside. Most shocking were glassed-in areas piled high with things like eyeglasses and hair clippings.

There are two parts to Auschwitz. A few kilometers away is Birkenau, where there are row upon row of barracks as well as the ruins of the crematorium. The barracks were haunting because they were left the way they were when the camp was liberated, packed with tiered bunk beds made of rough wood. It was easy to visualize the desperate people who had been imprisoned there.

The southeastern extreme of Mr. Sluggo's travels was Peloponnesia, the huge peninsula that's barely attached to mainland Greece – home of the ruins of ancient Corinth, Mycenae and Olympia.

That was part of the trip my father and I took. To get to Greece, we drove down the Yugoslav coast. The scenery was similar to Highway 1 in California but it was a pretty hairy ride because the road wasn't as good. Cars that had careened over the cliffs were left where they landed on the rocks below, their rusty hulks serving as safety reminders. Presumably the police had rescued the survivors or removed the bodies.

One pleasant stop along the Croatian coast was the walled city of Dubrovnik, which dates from the 7th Century. When Yugoslavia was disintegrating in the early 90s, it was disturbing to hear of the Serbs shelling the city.

Delphi was the most memorable of all the Greek ruins. The ancient city is the home of the Temple of Apollo. Both the ruins and the present day town are perched on the side of a mountain overlooking the Gulf of Corinth. At night, when the moon is bright, the whole area has a mystical aura.

Leaving Peloponnesia, we took a ferry from Patras across the Adriatic Sea to the Italian city of Brindisi. It was an 18-hour trip. We had a two-bunk cabin. I didn't know what the regulations were regarding dogs, so I didn't ask. I just carried Sluggo aboard under my arm.

We got in a quick walk just before the ship sailed that night. Sluggo was so well housebroken he would have exploded before having a so-called accident. He stayed in the cabin with us. When morning came, I took him to the rear deck where the cars were parked and sea water was splashing all over. I convinced him to lift his leg on a bicycle tire.

While we were waiting to disembark, a British woman noticed Sluggo and asked if I had had any trouble getting him aboard. I said no, because I didn't tell anybody. She snorted and walked away, no doubt thinking, "Crazy American."

The southwestern extreme for Mr. Sluggo was Arcachon, a seaside village near Bordeaux and the site of what is proclaimed to be the biggest sand dune in Europe. It may not be worth a trip just to climb the dune, but it's fun. On the steep ocean side were several German World War Two bunkers that were slowly sliding into the sea.

Italy was the only place I had a problem getting Sluggo into a hotel or motel. When my father and I visited Venice, we stayed at a hotel on the mainland. Dogs were forbidden, so Sluggo had to remain in the car overnight. Luckily he had outgrown his puppyhood habit of chewing things.

Most hotels in France charged an extra fee for dogs. Warras and I once stopped at a motel in a small town and noticed a sign on the door that said dogs were not allowed. He said, "Well, let's go." But I went in anyway, hoping to talk the owner into it. I didn't have to. Behind the desk was a sign in French that said: "Dogs - 10 Francs."

Further Travels with Warras

I traveled around Europe a number of times with Warras, whom I'd known since we worked together in the late 60s at WBBM-TV in Chicago, where we were both writer/producers. He was bitten by the travel bug while serving with the U.S. Army in Germany around 1960.

Warras was of average height with an expanding waistline and thinning hair crowning an oversized forehead. He wore glasses over his somewhat squinty eyes until getting Lasik surgery later in life.

Our travels took us all over Europe ranging from Sweden in the north to Istanbul in the east and as far southwest as Lourdes. Most of the time, we would travel in a car he had rented, splitting the cost of gas.

He got on my nerves once in a while, and I'm sure I annoyed him occasionally, but that's pretty much unavoidable with almost any traveling companion.

Jim was terrified of anyone in authority, which meant he always had his passport ready even if it wasn't necessary. Whenever we would approach an international border, he would have his left arm fully extended, gripping his passport between his thumb and fingertips. Most often, the guards would simply ignore him. Nevertheless, he'd stop and wave the passport in their faces until they motioned him on.

There was a time before Europe became borderless when Germany and Austria worked out an agreement for an express lane at their frontiers. The lane was designated by a green oval with a white E in the middle. It was for citizens of Germany or Austria who had nothing to declare.

As we neared the Austrian border, I figured we might as well use the express lane. The rental car had German license plates and we had nothing to declare, so I told Jim to aim for the E. A big mistake. Before I could say anything, he whipped out his passport. The guards got all excited and told us we had screwed up. But they waved us through after a few seconds, probably writing us off as dumb tourists. As we drove away, a flustered Jim complained, "You told me to get in the wrong lane."

I said nothing.

On another occasion, we were in Andorra, the tiny principality sandwiched between France and Spain, high in the snow-covered Pyrenees. The modern capital, Andorra la Vella, was very small with a population of only 15,000. It was crowded with high rises that appeared to be either apartments or condos.

Jim had never been to Spain, so after we looked around the city, he expressed an interest in driving to the Spanish border. He said he'd cross over, then immediately turn around, just so he could say he'd been there. I thought it was a stupid idea but he was driving so I couldn't object.

On an earlier trip, he had driven across the bridge linking the European corner of Turkey with the Asian part just so he could say he had driven all the way to Asia.

Jim wanted to make sure his passport was handy, so he pulled into a vacant lot next to a gas station on the edge of the city. Mr. Sluggo and I got out and walked around as he went through everything in the car, placing much of the contents on the ground. After about 20 minutes, he announced with an ashen face that he couldn't find his passport.

I was relieved that we weren't going to Spain.

We discussed what to do and decided to phone the motel where we had stayed the night before to ask if he had left his passport there. We'd been in the French city of Carcassone, located about three hours away.

We went to a large department store in the city center and found some pay phones outside the restaurant. I got a handful of coins, found the phone number in the motel directory we carried and called. A recording said the motel was closed until late afternoon.

Although we had been on our way to Lourdes, we decided to drive back to the motel and hope the passport was there.

As we left Andorra in the early afternoon, we were stopped by a French customs officer standing on the side of the road. Jim was noticeably nervous and borderline apoplectic because he didn't have his passport. Sensing something was wrong, the officer asked Jim to pop the trunk so he could search our luggage. After looking through the bags and the rest of the car, he asked to see the dog's inoculation record, which I had. Fortunately he never did ask for our passports.

Hours later back at the motel, Jim was stunned to learn that his passport had not been found. He ripped the car apart again. This time it turned up. It was in the map pocket along the base of the driver's door.

Our record for the slowest border crossing was one hour and 45 minutes going from Hungary into Romania.

Jim and I were three cars from the gate. The Romanians took our passports, looked through some of the luggage, helped themselves to a few cans of beer and confiscated a copy of *Newsweek* containing an article on then-President/Dictator Nicolae Ceausescu.

Suddenly all the guards disappeared except for one armed sentry. We waited. Nothing happened.

After half an hour, I spotted two Hungarian guards walking in the distance. I went up and asked if they knew where the Romanians were.

"Oh, yes," said one. "There's a football game on TV between Romania and England. They're all inside watching it. Perhaps they'll come out at halftime."

I related this to a German couple in the car behind us and the man quipped, "I hope Romania wins or we could be here forever."

Finally a guard came out. He returned our passports

and raised the gate. We didn't ask the score of the game.

Later on the same trip, we had two brushes with the law in Bulgaria. We'd been heading south, exploring the coast of the Black Sea, and had seen enough. Since I was the navigator, I noticed what looked like a much better road on the map that went straight to Turkey instead of zigzagging along the coast. I suggested we take it.

I dozed off before we got to the road. The next thing I knew, we were passing through a small town and almost everyone was waving, something that was very unusual.

After driving through open country, we came upon two young soldiers armed with rifles standing next to a guard house slightly larger than a phone booth. They motioned for us to stop. One of them went into the guard house and made a phone call, then the four of us stood around waiting and trying to communicate. It was hard to figure out what was going on because we couldn't seem to find a common language.

Finally, after more waiting and another phone call, they explained in a mixture of broken English and pantomime that we were to continue down the road a few kilometers until we came to an army base where we would "see the captain."

We drove to the base and were met outside the headquarters by the captain and a couple of soldiers. The captain explained that we were in a restricted military zone and asked if we had seen a certain sign back up the road. We each said we hadn't remembered any signs that said anything about a military zone. This was the mid-80s, the Iron Curtain still existed and Bulgaria was prepared for a NATO invasion from Turkey.

The captain turned us around with firm instructions to drive until we got back to the coastal road, then get on it.

Heading north again, we passed the back side of a large sign just before we reached the beach road. It measured at least six feet high and four feet wide. I asked Jim to stop so I could get a look at it.

Along with a big red "Do Not Enter" symbol, it said,

TRANSIT
VERBOTEN
FÜR AUSLÄNDER

That's German for Transit Forbidden for Foreigners. Lower on the sign, there was Turkish and Cyrillic writing, presumably saying the same thing.

I hadn't seen it because I'd been sleeping, but Jim knew enough German to understand the word *Verboten*. I asked why he had whizzed by. He said he had only noticed the word Transit and figured that meant driving through was OK.

We eventually got to Turkey after dark, almost kissing the ground as we crossed the border, and drove into a quiet little village. It was too late to try to go farther, so we found a hotel and checked in. It was one of the most Spartan places I'd ever seen but was remarkable for its low price. Splitting the tab, it was 65¢ each. The room was equipped with two simple beds and a wash basin. The toilet down the hall was squat style and truly grubby.

We went to a nearby restaurant where we were greeted as celebrities. Since there was no common language, the staff escorted us into the kitchen so we could point to what we wanted. And they tossed in things such as goat milk yogurt. The meal turned out to cost considerably more than the hotel. But it was good, filling and there were no aftereffects.

We played "see the captain" again after leaving Turkey and heading back through Bulgaria. This time, we were traveling on the main highway that ran northwest through Bulgaria and Yugoslavia, linking Turkey and Greece with Western Europe.

We stopped for a day to explore the Bulgarian capital, Sofia, then got back in the car to continue. Although we were heading northwest, Jim decided to backtrack to the southeast and catch the ring road so he could circle the city, thereby avoiding traffic. The ring was lopsided and the southeastern section was closest to the city center. I told Jim I thought driving northwest wouldn't be a problem since the city was compact and there wasn't much traffic. But he was driving, so we went southeast.

I advised him that when we got to the ring, he should get on it heading north, which would be to his left. When we reached it, I pointed out which road to take but he kept going straight.

As I was telling him we had to turn around, we came upon a police post, a wooden building on the side of the highway. Two policemen motioned for us to pull over. They asked for our passports, then went inside the building. We speculated on why we'd been stopped. I had no idea but Jim said he thought maybe it was because he was in the left lane and he should be in the right lane when approaching a police post.

I asked why he hadn't turned when I told him to. He said he was looking for a sign for Belgrade. I tried to explain there couldn't possibly be a sign for Belgrade because it was in the opposite direction.

We waited for what seemed to be forever. I leaned against the side of the car with my arms outstretched and my head tilted back, trying to soak up whatever sun made it through the Bulgarian haze.

After about an hour, I went inside and asked a policeman in German what was happening. He said we were being detained because we had transit visas and were going the wrong direction. He added that we had to wait to "see the captain," who was coming from somewhere else.

Wait we did. Finally the captain showed up. Before anyone could say anything, Jim launched into a detailed account of our entire day, starting with when we got up in the morning. He went on and on. When the captain got a chance to speak, he apologized for the delay. In flawless English, he said the police never should have detained us. He wished us a pleasant trip and we were on our way.

Less traveled roads

One of the best things about Cologne was its location. All of the Netherlands, Belgium and Luxembourg as well as the city of Paris were within a six hour drive. Denmark, Switzerland, Czechoslovakia and Britain could easily be reached in one day. I took advantage of this and did as much exploring as I could.

Every day I felt very fortunate to be living in Europe. I almost wanted to pinch myself to see if I was dreaming. Whenever I saw American tourists in the *Hauptbahnhof* fumbling with maps, guidebooks and luggage, I thought how terrific it was that I had all the time in the world to experience Europe, yet I could sleep in my "own bed" most nights.

Although I certainly haven't seen every beach in Europe, one of the best I came across was at Zandvoort, a Dutch resort near the city of Haarlem. There are fantastic sand dunes nearby. Zandvoort was very popular with Germans. Drinking songs echoed out of the bars.

Some of the most disappointing beaches in Europe were places along the French Riviera such as Nice and Cannes. There was plenty of glamour and high prices, but no sand. The beaches were composed of stones.

I stayed at the youth hostel in Nice on my very first visit to Europe nearly 20 years earlier. On the wall behind the check-in counter was a sign in English that said: "French Spoken Here."

Perhaps the strangest beach resort was the Italian town of Rimini, down the coast from Venice. During the mid-90s, it attracted large numbers of East Europeans who were hungry for travel following decades of restrictions under Communism. The main street, jammed with cruising cars, separated the narrow beach from an endless row of small hotels that looked like tenements. It was crowded and chaotic, hardly a good place to relax.

One thing that's fun to do is ride the steamships that sail around Lake Geneva (Lac Leman to French-speakers), which is sandwiched between eastern France and southwestern Switzerland. The sleek white boats are the aquatic equivalent of inter-city buses, linking Geneva with Lausanne, Montreux and other lakeside cities.

They've been around for quite a while. In his short story, *Miss King,* Somerset Maugham has his World War One British secret agent Mr. Ashenden commuting by ship between Geneva and the French city of Thonon on a dark and stormy night.

Another port of call in France is Evian, the town famous for its water. Evian is home to numerous spas where visitors can check in for health and beauty treatments, even for just a few hours.

Down the coast is Yvoire, an extremely photogenic medieval village where window boxes full of geraniums add a splash of color to the gray stone buildings.

For incredible sights, nothing beats the aforementioned Mont St. Michel. But Carcassonne finishes a close second. It's an ancient walled city in the far south of France that's reputed to be the best example of medieval fortification in existence. Two massive walls punctuated with 54 towers ring the city, which dates from the 5th century. It's not a ruin. People live there. For travelers who want to soak up the atmosphere, there are hotels and restaurants within the old city. When I first went there long ago, I stayed in the youth hostel, bought food in a nearby shop and cooked my own dinner, sharing the kitchen with other guests.

On one trip with my sister Jane, we stumbled upon a storybook 12th century castle at La Rochepot, a village near Beaune in the heart of Burgundy. Practically hidden in the forest, it had a drawbridge, plenty of turrets and costumed mannequins in some of the rooms.

Jim and I eventually made it to Lourdes, a city I had visited earlier on my own.

Whether a traveler believes in miracles or not, a visit to Lourdes is a fascinating experience. Located on the edge of the Pyrenees, the city attracts millions of pilgrims each year, most of whom are seeking a cure for some dreadful malady.

The Roman Catholic Church has certified only a handful of miracles over the years, meaning the odds of being cured are literally in the millions. But those odds are good enough to provide hope for the hopeless, and they keep coming.

The center of activity is the grotto where 14-year-old Bernadette Soubirous saw a vision of the Virgin Mary in 1858. Some of the sick arrive at the grotto in wheelchairs. Those in worse shape lie on gurneys pushed by nurses. There is a queue of people who want to light candles in front of a statue of the Virgin. Off on the side, others take turns at a long row of spigots, filling plastic jugs with spring water flowing from the grotto.

Lourdes abounds with souvenir shops and there's no limit to the tackiness. Not surprisingly, there's a large variety of religious statues for sale as well as the ubiquitous plastic water jugs. Easily the most outrageous item is the Blessed Virgin ashtray. Jim bought one – just to prove there was such a thing. He also stocked up on holy water.

In addition to the Louvre and other major sights in Paris, one offbeat attraction is Pére-Lachaise Cemetery, the final resting place of many famous people including Oscar Wilde, Sarah Bernhardt and a long list of exceptional artists who are so well known they need only one name: Piaf, Molière, Modigliani, Proust, Delacroix, Bizet and Hugo.

Even with a map of the cemetery, which is available at the administration building, finding certain graves isn't easy, partly because they're packed together so tightly. As I was wandering around, map in hand, a man walked up and asked,

"Have you seen Chopin?"

The most infamous grave is that of Jim Morrison, lead singer of the American rock group The Doors. He died in a Paris hotel of an apparent drug overdose in 1971. Fans have long been vandalizing Morrison's grave as well as nearby tombstones. There had been talk of moving him out of there, but at last report it hadn't happened.

The cemetery has been a popular sight for a long, long time. Mark Twain wrote about it in his book *The Innocents Abroad,* published in 1869. He described it as one of his "pleasantest visits" in Paris.

A truly macabre Parisian adventure is a walk through the Catacombs where millions of skeletons from various cemeteries were consolidated in 1785. It's shocking at first but you become immune after seeing the first thousand skulls.

Speaking of the macabre: in the Dutch capital, The Hague, is a museum dedicated to medieval instruments of torture such as the iron maiden. Called *Gevangenpoor,* it's located in the city center.

For a concentration camp that's more on the beaten track than Auschwitz, there's Mauthausen, located near the Austrian city of Linz.

Mauthausen is among the best-preserved of any of the camps I've seen. Many of the buildings are still standing and some barracks have been reconstructed. The exhibits are more interesting than most. Between 1938 and 1945, an estimated 225,000 prisoners lived and died there, many of them laboring at an adjacent stone quarry.

My sister and I stopped off at Linz while traveling by train from Munich to Vienna. We couldn't find any way to get to the camp by public transport, so we hired a taxi, which was quite expensive.

Two larger camps – Dachau, outside Munich, and Buchenwald, near the eastern German city of Weimar – are impressive but Mauthausen had more of a creepy feeling for me.

At Bergen-Belsen, where Anne Frank died, there are memorials and an exhibition center, but nothing remains of the original buildings. British troops torched the camp after liberating it because it was infected with typhus, which is what killed Anne Frank.

One place that struck me as especially creepy was the Ploetzensee Memorial in Berlin. Ploetzensee is a small prison where political prisoners were held during the war. It was designated as a memorial to the German Resistance because that's where 100 conspirators and dissidents were hanged following the failed assassination attempt on Hitler on July 20, 1944.

I'd never heard of Ploetzensee until I wound up there covering a *Kranzniederlegung* (Remember that word from page 54?) conducted by Chancellor Kohl. The most chilling feature was the execution room where a row of meat hooks hung from a rusty pipe.

Just as disturbing as any concentration camp are the ruins of Oradour-sur-Glane, a French village 12 miles northwest of Limoges that was destroyed by German troops on June 10, 1944.

Oradour fell victim to elements of a Panzer division that had been racing northward to help counter the Normandy invasion. The troops killed everyone they could find – 642 people – then set fire to every building.

In the worst incident, they herded at least 400 women and children into the church and killed most of them with guns and grenades. Then they tossed wood and straw into the building and set it on fire. Anyone who survived the shooting was burned alive. A melted church bell is testament to the intense heat.

As a memorial, everything was left the way it was that day, frozen in time. Streetcar tracks that connected with Limoges wind their way between the shells of homes and shops lining the main street. Scattered here and there are rusting cars and twisted bicycles. Inside the homes are pots and pans and other furnishings. At the tailor shop is a rusting sewing machine.

Visiting the village cemetery and seeing tiny photos of the victims on their tombstones puts a human face on that tragic day.

Although there's no shortage of theories on why Oradour was targeted, historians can't agree on a specific reason.

The countryside of northern France and southern Belgium is dotted with dozens of cemeteries and memorials honoring Commonwealth troops who gave their lives in World War One. The most imposing monument is the Canadian war memorial at Vimy Ridge, located just a few miles north of the French town of Arras. Twin limestone pylons soar into the air to serve as a tribute to the 66,000 Canadians killed during the Great War.

The battle of Vimy Ridge was especially nasty. On April 9, 1917, 20,000 Canadian troops stormed the ridge, which was a key part of the German defenses. Within hours, they had captured the crest, but suffered casualties of more than 50%.

Near the memorial are sand-bagged trenches and tunnels left pretty much as they were nearly 100 years ago. In some places, the opposing trenches where Canadian and British troops fought the Germans are so close that a soldier could almost reach across and touch fingertips with the enemy.

During the summer, young Canadian guides working for the Veterans Affairs office lead tours of the tunnels. One of the interesting things they point out is the tip of an unexploded artillery shell sticking through the roof of a tunnel. Immediately after that shell hit, troops dug the tunnels deeper.

One little-known reminder of both the First and

Second World Wars is a Belgian fort named Breendonk. Located between Brussels and Antwerp, it was built between 1906 and 1914 for the defense of Antwerp.

However, it was captured by the Germans in both wars. Between 1940 and 1944 it was used as a mini concentration camp. Visitors can see the cells where the prisoners were kept, as well as the torture and execution areas.

Gyrations

Under new management

It was early 1988, about six months before my contract was due to expire. Rex announced he was going to quit and move to Hong Kong to look for a job. That meant a new producer would be needed.

I mentioned this to my friend Jim Warras, who was working at KNBC in Burbank, and asked if he knew of any producers who might want a job in Europe. I knew it was a long shot, but it would be terrific to have an American who knew what he was doing producing the show.

Some weeks later, a guy named Larry Levin turned up inquiring about the job. Larry was thin, bald and always blinking and squinting. He said he had worked at KNBC, but I never put two and two together and realized I may have been partly responsible for the fact that he was in Cologne. Assuming he was an experienced producer, I gladly filled him in about Rex and all the other *European Journal* oddities.

I asked Warras and Doug Culver, a KNBC producer, about Larry and each said, "Oh, he's OK." Not a ringing endorsement, but they didn't put him down either.

Larry, who apparently was the only candidate, got the job. Unfortunately, it soon became apparent that he probably had never produced a show before.

Larry was so hyper he quickly earned the nickname *Das Eichhörnchen* – German for squirrel.

By that time, the reporters' office had been moved to another floor and consisted of two rooms. There was a large one with a number of desks to accommodate an intern and occasional appearances by freelancers. Off to one side was a smaller room Jerry Huffman and I shared.

One of the first things Larry did was banish Jerry to the

larger room and commandeer his desk. Partly in sympathy with Jerry and partly because I didn't want Larry as a roommate, I moved out too. Neil the anchorman took over my desk.

As producer, Larry got to approve story ideas and scripts. After reading one of my scripts, he questioned the fact that it had two standups – a rarity for me. I told him it didn't matter how many standups there were as long as it made sense. Larry poked his head into the larger room and asked, "Anybody ever heard of a story with two standups?" Everyone ignored him. He turned to me and said, "Cut one."

Larry would often disappear for a day or two but never told anyone, including Rendelsmann, that he'd be gone. And Rendelsmann would become unhinged whenever he couldn't find him.

One day, there were several of us in the office. My phone rang. It was Rendelsmann, very agitated. "Where's that Larry Levin?" he asked.

"I don't know," I said. "I haven't seen him."

I cupped my hand over the phone and asked, "Anyone know where Larry is?"

"No."

I told him nobody knew.

Seconds later, the phone rang on another desk. It was Rendelsmann asking the same question. Then he rang a third phone. We all thought he had lost his mind.

On one occasion when Larry was missing all day, he turned up on the TV news that evening. There was a story about a high profile trial in Düsseldorf. The video showed a lawyer talking with reporters outside the courthouse. Standing among them was Larry. We cued up the tape of the newscast and gave it to Rendelsmann. I don't know if he watched it.

Rumors circulated that Larry had been moonlighting as a field producer for NBC News.

In another case, Larry's picture appeared in the daily paper the day after he had disappeared. He was in a group photo with Jane Fonda somewhere in East Germany. We made sure the paper got to Rendelsmann's desk. Once again, there was no way of knowing how he reacted, but at least it answered the question, "Where's that Larry Levin?"

Jerry Huffman and I maintained our sanity by concentrating on our stories and trying to ignore all the craziness in the office. As much as we enjoyed our jobs, it was often so wacky we were almost relieved that our contracts were nearing an end.

Back to the USA

Before my contract expired, I met with Rendelsmann and Werner Hadulla of Transtel to discuss my future. Hadulla was a large man with dark hair. He had a low forehead and pug nose topped with plastic-framed glasses, bearing a slight resemblance to Garrison Keillor of Lake Wobegon fame. He treated me all right, so I respected him.

Hadulla said I could either start my own company "like Mary Beth" or return to the United States, get a temporary job, then rejoin *European Journal* nine months later. The reason he insisted I get a job elsewhere was to prove once again that I had made a clean break with the company and wasn't just waiting in the wings to return.

I chose the second option because I didn't want the hassle of setting up my own company. That would have required hiring a European, actually an accountant who could handle all the German paperwork. However, he or she would have been listed as the head of the company because foreigners weren't allowed to run businesses in Germany. In other words, as far as the government was concerned, my assistant would be my boss. It sounded like a giant can of worms, and besides, I wanted to be a reporter not a businessman.

Even though I loved the job, I needed a break and thought it would be nice to return to the USA for a while. Giving up my apartment was no problem because I'd been in it for nearly five years and felt it was time to find a better place. The truck had started to rust out on the front fenders – normal for a Renault 4 – and it needed to be replaced, so getting rid of it fit in with my plans.

Word got out that I wanted to sell the truck. An American who freelanced at the radio station expressed interest, so I sold it to him for 1,500 DM after originally having paid 5,000. The truck had traveled 92,000 km, meaning I had put 70,000 km on it or about 11,000 miles each year for four years, mostly for fun.

I couldn't complain about the truck's durability. The only repair it ever needed was a brake job.

I later heard the guy who bought the truck had totaled it on the autobahn. But he wasn't hurt. I pictured the cleanup crew using shovels to scoop up all the rust.

I reluctantly put my household things in storage in Cologne and returned to the USA in August of 1988. First, I picked up my car, a 1980 Chevy Citation that was occupying part of my sister Lynn's driveway in Olathe, Kansas. Then I drove to California, stopping at my sister Jane's place in Walnut Creek, east of San Francisco.

By sheer luck, I found out from Warras that KNBC happened to be looking for a temporary writer to fill out the vacation schedule. I drove to Burbank, met with the executive producer, Peter O'Connell, and was hired. I knew nothing about computers because we had standard typewriters at *European Journal*, so O'Connell gave me a one hour crash course. Days of training would have been much better.

One thing that apparently worked in my favor was the fact that I had been a vacation relief writer at KNBC nearly 10 years earlier and still knew some of the people there. That may be why I didn't have to take the dreaded writing test.

Warras had an extra room at his house, so Mr. Sluggo and I stayed there rent-free. Things were working out much better than I could have expected. I had the required temporary job and was collecting pay stubs to prove it.

The work at KNBC was routine, writing scripts for 20 second voiceovers, often with very little information to go on, or shepherding a package through the editing process, which usually proceeded on autopilot. There was little to do other than retype a lead-in and make sure all the fonts had correct numbers. It was a well-oiled news machine.

While I was there, I learned that Larry Levin had worked as a writer and an assistant on the assignment desk but had never produced anything. When I asked Warras and Culver why they hadn't warned me about Larry, each said he really didn't know much about him because he hadn't worked directly with him. That made sense. Actually, the copy editor would be the best judge of any writer. The producers and other writers saw the material only after it was processed.

By coincidence, Tom Hayden had just published his autobiography, a book called *Reunion,* and Levin was mentioned in it. Hayden was a 1960s student radical and member of the Chicago Seven who had been married to Jane Fonda for many years. He later served in both the California State Assembly and State Senate.

When Hayden first met Levin, he described him as "a burnt-out Bobby Kennedy worker" living in Venice, California, who was "bald at 25, Jewish, and a student dropout."

Judging from the book, Larry was a lifelong political activist. Hayden wrote that he was in Northern Ireland in 1969 helping the Catholics with their civil rights movement. In 1972, he "flew an emergency relief mission" to Wounded Knee, South Dakota, to help members of the American Indian Movement who were in a standoff with federal marshals. And in 1974, he was in Washington, D.C., directing the Coalition to Stop Funding the (Vietnam) War.

While I was still at KNBC, I wrote to Hadulla and asked how everything looked for the next year. He said he didn't know and suggested once again that I consider setting up my own business in Cologne.

When the job ended in November, I returned to my sister Jane's place to pick up some things. Optimistic that everything would eventually work out in Cologne, Mr. Sluggo and I headed to the Jersey Shore to relax until it was time to return. Longtime friends Bill and Marianne Klink owned two Victorian houses in Cape May that they rented out during the summer. Since the houses sat vacant in winter, they said I could stay in one providing I paid for the heating oil. That was no small thing because the houses were three stories high and drafty.

It was fun living in a resort during the off season. The weather changed constantly, sometimes cold, sometimes rainy, once or twice a couple feet of snow, which Sluggo really loved. On Thanksgiving weekend, the weather was so warm and sunny that half the population of Philadelphia turned up on the beach.

I checked the trade journals and halfheartedly applied for a few jobs, although I knew I could never find anything as good as reporting for *European Journal*. Regardless of the weather, Mr. Sluggo and I spent most of the time walking, exploring all of Cape May by foot.

I wrote to Rendelsmann early in the New Year, 1989, and asked what was happening regarding my return. He replied that he wasn't sure and said I might want to seek long-term employment in the United States. By then, Hadulla had retired after suffering a stroke, so he was out of the picture.

I hadn't been concerned because everything went without a hitch following the interim arrangement with Strastil. And although Rendelsmann and I could never be described as friends, we had always had a good relationship. I was closer to him than any boss I'd ever had. And as far as I knew, I'd never done anything that had him bouncing off the walls as Rex, Larry and others had.

But eventually the job evaporated. It appeared that when they promised I could return, they never gave any thought as to whether it would actually be possible.

I didn't want to stay on the East Coast, so I wrote to all the San Francisco TV stations and asked whether they used freelancers. Two stations said yes, so I drove back to California in March and camped out at my sister's condo.

I wound up freelancing at three different stations, most often KPIX, followed by KRON and KTVU in Oakland.

KPIX and KRON had different computer systems, so I took notes which I referred to every time I sat down in order to keep things straight. KTVU didn't have a computer. It was just like the old days, ripping multilayered paper out of the typewriter and starting over every time I made a mistake.

Since I was "the new guy" at each place, I got the least important things to do, so it was pretty much drudgery, a real letdown after traveling all over Europe as a reporter.

After some months, I wound up working exclusively at KPIX. My erratic schedule usually had me going in one or two days each week. Sometimes I worked a 40-hour week. Sometimes zero.

The dreaded writing test & a bizarre interview

I kept checking the trade journals for real jobs. In the summer of 1989, Radio Free Europe ran a display ad in *Broadcasting* magazine announcing that writer/editors were being recruited for the Munich headquarters. My first thought was, "Hey, if I can get this, I'll be back in Germany, in-country, and have a much better shot at *European Journal*."

I applied and was invited to Washington, D.C. for an interview.

I arrived in D.C. on the Fourth of July for an appointment the next morning. I hadn't been there for years and had forgotten how incredibly hot and muggy it is in midsummer.

Turning up at the RFE building on Connecticut Avenue, I had expected to find a busy newsroom, but the place was practically deserted.

I met with Tom Bodin, chief of the Washington News Bureau, and Barry Griffiths, who worked in the News and Current Affairs Division in Munich. Bodin was a large guy who was very personable. Griffiths was thin with large glasses and sandy hair.

After the three of us discussed the job, Griffiths administered the writing test. I hoped I had reached the point where I'd never have to take another test, but no such luck. He sat me down at a computer in a windowless, dimly-lit room and told me I'd be writing half a dozen stories from wire copy. He wanted each to run about 20 seconds.

I had one hour to complete the work. I finished much sooner, saved the stories in the computer and alerted Griffiths. He glanced over the material, then told me one particular story about a Gorbachev speech should be longer because he wanted an in-depth piece.

I touched it up, adding another 20 seconds, but Griffiths said it was still too short. So I made it even longer. It turned out to be a full page.

He finally accepted the story, then asked if I had any questions. I did: "What's a typical work schedule like?"

I couldn't believe his answer: "I'm sure you'd find the work schedule better suited for a younger man."

I didn't react, but filed his comment away in the back of my head, hoping it might prove useful in the future.

Quake!

Back in California, I continued working at KPIX and happened to be in the building when the big 7.1 earthquake struck on October 17, 1989.

It was 5:04 p.m. The news had just started. I was standing in the newsroom when I felt the building start rumbling. I immediately dove under one of the steel desks. Everyone else I could see froze in place. The grinding vibration lasted 15 seconds. Then it was quiet.

The KPIX building was on the side of a hill overlooking the Embarcadero. It was only a few stories high and sturdy as a bunker, so there was no apparent damage. But the electricity had been knocked out, meaning we weren't broadcasting. After a short time, the emergency generator kicked in. Camera crews and reporters were dispatched all over the area to do nonstop live shots.

Since everything was being improvised, many of the people in the newsroom had little to do except watch the quake coverage on TV.

I was wondering how I was going to get back to Walnut Creek since the Bay Bridge was impassable and the BART trains that ran under the bay were stopped pending an inspection. One of the reporters did a piece about ferry boats transporting people from the Embarcadero across the bay to Jack London Square in Oakland. I decided to try that.

Even though the news director said he wanted everyone to stick around, I saw no sense in doing so because I hadn't done anything for six hours. I told the 11 p.m. producer, who also had nothing to do, that I was taking off. I left at my normal time, 11:15.

It was eerie being in a big city in complete darkness. I walked the few blocks down to the Embarcadero and, sure enough, there was a large boat waiting. Dozens of people formed a line, inching toward the boat, which was already packed. A short time later, the boat steamed across the bay. As we sailed under the Bay Bridge, everyone peered upward, trying to spot the damage. Nothing unusual was noticeable.

A long row of buses stood by at Jack London Square. Signs on the front of each indicated they were bound for various BART stations. I got on one destined for mine and about half an hour later I was there. It was amazing how efficient the system was. And it didn't cost anything.

Back in the condo, the quake had knocked a few small things to the floor, but there was no real damage.

My sister, who usually returned home in the early evening, didn't show up until well after midnight. She also worked in San Francisco and had gotten into a car pool that had to detour across the Golden Gate Bridge and travel around the north end of the bay.

By the next afternoon, BART had been declared safe and I commuted to KPIX as usual.

It took several days before electricity was completely restored in the Bay Area. In the hours immediately following the quake, when most of San Francisco was dark, the TV stations presumably had a very small audience watching their Herculean efforts.

Perhaps more frightening than the earthquake itself were the aftershocks. While the quake was a rumbling sensation, the aftershocks were big, quick jolts. When one of them hit, it felt as if a giant hand from deep inside the Earth had slapped the surface. There was always suspense afterwards, wondering if and when the next one would come.

The jolts continued sporadically for weeks.

Fighting back

Several weeks later, I received a letter from Radio Free Europe dated November 2. It said, "Thanks for your interest ... We've selected and made offers to other applicants whose qualifications and skills more closely match our needs."

That was my cue to fight back. I wrote to RFE saying I was disappointed but not surprised that I hadn't been hired. I quoted Barry Griffiths' statement about the work schedule being better suited for a younger man, saying I thought it was odd that RFE would practice age discrimination when experienced writers presumably were much in demand.

Everything hit the fan in Washington. A couple of weeks later, I received a two-page letter from the personnel director saying Mr. Griffiths did "not remember making the remark in question," but nevertheless a "thorough investigation" had been launched.

At the end of the letter, he noted that the Munich news director would be in California in January. He said if I wanted to meet with him "to discuss future openings," I should contact the personnel office to set up an appointment.

I wasted no time in calling. I learned that the news director, Ken Thompson, would be visiting relatives in Capistrano Beach for a few days in January. Fortunately, I happened to have longtime friends there, so I made the appointment and arranged to stay with them.

I drove to Capistrano, about one hour south of LA, and met Thompson at a crowded restaurant the next morning for a late breakfast. I was dressed in a gray flannel suit. He was dressed in a gray sweat suit. He said I shouldn't have dressed up. I was glad I had.

Thompson was tall and thin, bearing a vague resemblance to the actor James Cromwell, who played the farmer in *Babe* and the corrupt police captain in *LA Confidential*. We talked about RFE for a while, then I asked the burning question: "Why was I rejected?"

"Because you didn't follow the instructions for the writing test."

I was puzzled. I asked for an explanation. He said the problem was that I had made one story considerably longer than the others. I pointed out that I had been specifically instructed to make that story as long as it was.

It was obvious what had happened. I was the first person interviewed and Griffiths apparently decided to dispense with the in-depth story for subsequent candidates but forgot to tell whoever reviewed the copy.

Shortly before meeting Thompson, I had managed to land a three-week job at Blue Danube Radio and I'd be going to Vienna in mid-February, one month away. I mentioned this to him and offered to swing through Munich so I could reapply at RFE. He agreed.

Another shot at Cologne

I arranged to fly to Frankfurt, then travel by train to Vienna so I could stop in Munich. But first I wanted to remind Rendelsmann that I wanted my old job back.

From the airport, I went to Bonn to check in with my friend Chris Wright and his German wife Evelin. Chris was from Lima, Ohio and had worked for *European Journal* as a freelancer when I was under contract. He later got a contract of his own. After that ended, he started his own TV production business in Cologne – in partnership with a German guy.

The next day, I walked into the *Deutsche Welle*, unannounced. I phoned Rendelsmann from the reception desk. He was in. He surprised me by asking if I could come up in an hour for a "big meeting." I said, "Sure."

I killed time pacing around outside the cafeteria, then headed to his office. We went up a few floors and met with Dr. Ulrich Schaeffer of Transtel and Ulrich von Thuna, Hadulla's replacement.

I had known Dr. Schaeffer from the beginning but not very well. He was a slight man with rimless glasses and thinning hair, always well-dressed. Von Thuna, who I'd never seen before, was a larger man, very business-like.

They spoke with me about producing the show. Although I preferred working as a reporter, I saw producing as a way of getting back on the staff.

At one point, Rendelsmann expressed fear that I might soften the show. I told him it was already too soft and needed to be more topical. He may have been thinking of my Paris pooper scooper story, which I looked upon as environmental, or the 2CV story, which I considered to be of social and economic significance, not fluff. In any case, my serious stories far outnumbered the lighter ones.

After an hour of discussion, von Thuna stood up and said, "Fine. We'll send you a written offer."

I asked myself, "Did they just hire me or what?"

As Rendelsmann and I walked back to his office, he stopped in the hall three times to talk with various people. Each time, he pointed to me and said, "You're looking at the next producer of *European Journal*."

Each person congratulated me.

"Hey," I thought, "They really did hire me!"

Even though it looked as if the job was in the bag, I decided it was best to go ahead with the appointment at Radio Free Europe, just in case.

RFE was located in a former hospital on the northeast side of Munich. It was a long, low, white building hugging the edge of an enormous park called the English Garden. They booked me into a small hotel nearby.

The next morning, I saw Thompson along with Griffiths and a number of other people. Unlike Washington, the Munich newsroom was humming with activity.

Unfortunately I had to take the dreaded writing test again. Then it was on to Vienna.

Beautiful Blue Danube

After I learned I had the job in Vienna, I contacted Jerry Huffman, who was back in Wisconsin. He gave me the name of a woman who had a room to rent. I made arrangements with her before leaving California and went directly to the apartment. Although Jerry had raved about the place, I didn't care for it at all. It was one simple room with the bathroom down the hall. No kitchen.

Once at Blue Danube, I learned of a woman who was looking for a renter. I called and arranged to see the place after work. It was dark when I got to the address. I thought I might be at the wrong building because it was so shabby on the outside. But I got up the courage to walk up one floor and found the apartment. It was fantastic. I took it immediately.

The woman was a travel agent who had moved in with her boyfriend but didn't want to give up her own place. The apartment was two large rooms overlooking the street, packed with furniture and plants. Squeezed into alcoves in each room were built-in double bunk beds. There was a separate eat-in kitchen plus a small bathroom. I got out of the first apartment and moved in the next day.

My primary job at Blue Danube was reading the news for half an hour at 6 p.m., plus doing a five minute update at 7. With no commercials, there was a lot of reading, even with sound bites and reporter packages.

Earlier in the day, I either hosted a variety show from 10 a.m. to noon or another show from 2 to 4 that featured easy listening records and CDs with minimal talk.

The morning show included a little bit of everything from recorded music to reading funny stories off the wires to talking with the British recipe lady who came in to explain how to make dishes such as chile con carne. As far as that show went, it was obvious I was not in the same league as the lively, fast-talking British disc jockeys.

After a few days, I met with the boss, a tall, attractive blonde named Tilia Harald. I asked how I was doing. She described my work as a news reader as "outstanding" but indicated I might be the worst talk show host in the history of radio. They quickly revised the schedule, removing me from hosting duties and limiting my non-news work to introducing records. No complaints from me.

After the first week, I wrote to Rendelsmann and asked if I should stop in Cologne before returning to the U.S. He replied very quickly, saying there was no need for another visit; they might even send the offer before I left Vienna.

They didn't.

Even though I worked only a few hours each day and it was fun, 21 days without a break really wore me down. After about two weeks, it seemed as if it would never end.

EJ slips away

Finishing at Blue Danube, I found a cheap flight to London and flew there for job interviews at CNN and ABC News. Then I swung through Paris by train en route to Frankfurt to see an American who had his own production house. No offers were forthcoming.

To make matters worse, I returned to California to find my freelance work had dried up. While I was away, KPIX management decided to stop using freelancers and actually hire writers. Although I had told the assistant news director I'd be back in a month, I somehow got lost in the shuffle.

Meanwhile, the offer from Rendelsmann never appeared. Another query brought a response that it was taking the "big bosses" longer than expected to formulate their offer.

A few more weeks passed and I wrote again. This time, I got an astounding answer: "Be patient. There are other candidates."

It looked like big trouble, so I contacted the University of California at Berkeley and hired a translator so I could fire off letters in proper German.

First I wrote to Rendelsmann. I said if he followed through with the plan to rehire me, I'd give him a good show with "no angst, no stress and no chaos" – three things that had often been staples at *European Journal*.

I also sent a letter to von Thuna asking what had happened to the job, noting that Rendelsmann had been introducing me as the "next producer."

I got a quick reply from him. Amazingly, he said the

meeting was just a "get-acquainted" session and he hadn't promised anything.

When I heard from Rendelsmann, he said they hadn't yet decided what to do but he hoped to get back to me soon.

He didn't.

A short time later, word reached me that the job had been given to an American woman who had contributed stories to *European Journal* on rare occasions. The only consolation for me was that she didn't last long.

Strangely enough, I wasn't upset about being replaced because I'd been skeptical all along, thinking, "I'll believe it when I see it."

What did bother me was that Rendelsmann didn't have to courtesy to notify me that I'd been dumped.

Surprise, you're hired

In June, out of the blue, I received a letter from Radio Free Europe offering me a job, which I immediately accepted. It was just in time because I really needed the work and the money.

Sluggo and I left California and drove to my brother Ed's place in Kansas where I assembled things I wanted to ship to Germany and sold my aging car to my nephew.

On July 11, 1990 – one year and one week after the initial interview in Washington – we flew to Germany. It was my last time on Pan Am before it went belly up, and I traveled in style. While changing planes in New York, I managed to talk my way into business class. The ground staff apparently became sympathetic when they saw my one-way ticket cost $995. RFE reimbursed me of course.

One of the best things about RFE was that the company provided furnished apartments for its imported employees, and virtually everything but a toothbrush was included. RFE also paid the rent, which was added to the employee's salary for tax purposes.

After landing in Munich, I hopped in a taxi, swung by RFE to pick up my key and went to the apartment. The folks in personnel had asked my preference in advance. I told them I'd like to be within one kilometer of the office on the ground floor of an older building.

But that wasn't the way it turned out. I was on the sixth and highest floor of a boxy postwar building in the heart of Schwabing, a district known as Munich's Greenwich Village. There was a lot of traffic and sirens and very little greenery. Even worse, there was sap falling from the trees that made the sidewalks sticky.

As expected, the apartment was completely furnished with dishes, pots and pans, bedding and even an iron, an ironing board and a vacuum cleaner. But the place was a bit worn and somewhat dreary.

Balconies were common but this one was frightening. It was tacked onto the kitchen on the backside of the building, measuring slightly more than one square yard. It overlooked a parking lot – nice view – and the wrought iron railing looked so flimsy I didn't want to touch it.

RFE regulations said anyone who didn't like the first apartment could change, so I looked at another place in a totally different neighborhood. I really liked it and moved as soon as I could, with RFE handling the move and picking up the tab.

The second apartment was in a three-block-long building that was so new the far end was still under construction. It was five stories high and I was on the middle floor. Even though the building was monstrous, it was divided into units to make it seem small. When I got off the elevator, there were doors to only four apartments.

At nearly 600 square feet, the apartment was roomy enough. It was L-shaped like the one in Cologne. Upon entering, there was a hallway with the bathroom immediately on the left. About 10 feet further on the left was the kitchen, which was large enough to squeeze in a small table and two chairs. Two doors side-by-side at the end of the hall opened into the bedroom and living room.

Unlike the apartment in Schwabing, this one was in perfect shape and all the furniture was new, although the refrigerator was once again a Ken and Barbie model. Compared with the simple accommodations I had in Cologne, the place was luxurious. The furnishings included nice touches like little tables with lamps on either side of the bed and windows covered by sheer curtains as well as heavy draperies.

On entering the living room, there was a dining table with four chairs directly beneath a ceiling lamp, and a tall bookcase against the opposing wall. Covering much of the wall to the right was a group of modular cabinets similar to what I had in Cologne. They faced a couch on the opposite side of the room with an oval coffee table in between. In front of a picture window at the end of the room was a love seat. There was a square table with lamp in the left corner.

To the right of the window, a glass door opened onto a sturdy concrete balcony as wide as the apartment. It overlooked a grassy courtyard with a gazebo in the middle.

There were washers and dryers in the basement, so I didn't have to find a laundromat or buy my own machines. Also in the basement, or *Keller,* and typical of a German apartment building, were individual storage areas – not rooms but cages, almost like jail cells.

The bedroom had the customary *Schrank.* One thing that was missing was a chest of drawers. There was no place to put socks, underwear and other folded items. I asked the housing office if that was an oversight. The answer was yes. I was told I could go to one of the big department stores, pick out a chest and bill it to RFE, which I did.

The new apartment was farther from RFE and necessitated taking a bus and a *Strassenbahn* if I didn't use my bike, which I had shipped over as part of my personal effects. It took 20 minutes by bike vs. twice that long on public transit, so I always pedaled to work, weather permitting.

I never seriously considered buying a car, mainly because Munich was too far from my old haunts near Cologne. No more one hour drives to Belgium. Whenever I wanted to get away, I rented a car.

The new neighborhood was close to being on the northern edge of the suburbs and therefore was much quieter and had more open space. My kitchen and bedroom windows overlooked a field which was planted with either corn or sunflowers or nothing, depending on the season.

RFE also paid to get my household articles out of storage in Cologne.

One of the first things I did when everything arrived was take my down comforter to a shop to have it cleaned. It's customary to get that done every five years.

The man in the shop explained that what they do is remove the feathers and wash them. I asked why they didn't just wash the whole thing. He said because the cover was *imprägniert* or impregnated, meaning waterproof. If that were the case, I wondered, why do we need to clean the feathers anyway? But I figured they knew what they were doing, so I gave the go-ahead. The man agreed to send the cover to a dry cleaner while the feathers were being washed.

Munich had a lot more style than Cologne. The city had plenty of parks and museums and old buildings that were either untouched by the war or carefully restored. The hilly Olympic Park, where the 1972 games were held, was built on top of war debris that was hauled away from the city center.

Bicycles were a popular means of transportation in Munich as well as other Bavarian cities. There were bike paths everywhere and motorists actually tried to avoid hitting the cyclists. Bikes seemed to be much more common in Munich than Cologne.

The world-famous *Oktoberfest* is a real spectacle. With its huge, crowded, noisy beer halls, it's one of those attractions that's really fun the first time but gets stale fast when out-oftowners turn up looking for an escort.

One of the more unusual things about Munich is a meteorological oddity called the *Föhn* (pronounced fern), which is also slang for a hair dryer. The *Föhn* is a warm, dry wind that pushes over the Alps from the Mediterranean and makes many people feel awful, even on the sunniest days. Some complain of insomnia, others say it makes their sinuses act up and still others suffer from back pain. It made me dizzy. The only good thing about the *Föhn* is that it usually doesn't affect people until they've lived in Munich for a while.

Getting down to work

I was looking forward to working at Radio Free Europe because of the historic role it played in the Cold War, broadcasting untainted news to people behind the Iron Curtain. The nerve center was in a large room called NCA – the News and Current Affairs office. All the English-speaking writers worked there, compiling newscasts 24 hours a day, 365 days a year.

NCA was on the back side of a long curved building that skirted the edge of the enormous 18th century English Garden. Not far away was an open air beer garden that seated thousands. When the weather was nice and the windows were cracked open, laughing and singing could be heard.

RFE got most of its news from the Associated Press, Reuters, Agence France Presse and the Soviet news agency TASS as well as some obscure East Bloc agencies. The material came in on teletype machines. Major wires also were fed into the computer. Additional information was provided by reporters and freelancers in the field.

There were endless files. Just below the windows lining the outside wall were two tiers of rollout drawers that seemed to contain every script ever written. Going through those sometimes-crumbling old scripts to verify facts was frustrating and tedious, but being accurate was by far the most important aspect of the job.

The Russians prepared their newscasts in the same room. Management had moved them in so we could work closely together because Russia was the most important area of influence. Occasionally there would be a news item from TASS in Russian that we needed for the general wire. In that case, one of the Russians would stand next to a writer and dictate an English translation. Then the writer would try to make sense of it.

Except during the overnight hours and weekend mornings, there were at least four people working on the newscasts. The person calling the shots was the supervising editor. He would select stories and assign them to the writers. There were usually two of them. The fourth person worked what was known as "the slot," clearing the teletypes, writing, editing copy and helping the editor.

Unlike AP, UPI or other radio news services, NCA did not produce a fresh newscast every hour. Instead, stories were written and updated continuously. Once a story was written, it was sent throughout the building by teletype and translated into 22 languages covering an area from the Baltic States through Central Asia to the Soviet Far East.

Fifteen minutes before each hour, the slot editor would put out a list of the top stories as a guide for the various "desks," as they were called. Compared with the commercial broadcasting world, there was little pressure.

As far as style was concerned, we were supposed to write as simply as possible to make it easy on the translators. One particular thing we had to do was change a title with the word "vice" in it to "deputy," except in the case of the U.S. vice president. Apparently there was some fear that vice mayor might be translated as mayor of vice.

The news was a mix of major stories from around the world as well as important developments from the coverage area. RFE went big on the Gulf War and the disintegration of

Yugoslavia. When Boris Yeltsin stood on a tank in August, 1991 to challenge a coup against Mikhail Gorbachev, it was a monster story.

The worst job in the office, in my opinion, was being assigned to CMD, the Central Monitoring Desk – a desk that handled secondary news, most of which came from minor news agencies in English that was difficult to understand. The possibility of making a mistake was always hanging over the writer's head. In fact, one day a man from one of the desks burst through the door waving a piece of CMD copy, yelling, "Wrong, wrong!"

Fortunately I was not the author.

It turned out the work schedule wasn't especially suited for people of any age. There were several morning shifts that started anywhere between 7:30 and 10:30, afternoon shifts that started at either 2 or 3:30 and an evening shift that ran from 7 p.m. to 3 a.m. Most shifts totaled eight hours with a lunch break included, meaning we almost always worked a 35 hour week. To make things even better, NCA had a policy that once a month each writer got a three-day weekend.

Despite generous paychecks (veteran writers were said to be earning at least $100,000 a year) and a liberal amount of vacation (in addition to six weeks off plus comp time, RFE observed both German and American holidays), morale was low. Many staffers had little respect for the people running the place, complaining they didn't know what they were doing.

When I started, the senior editor was Dan Williams, a thin, bespectacled blonde-haired guy from Oklahoma. Dan was well-liked. He treated everyone courteously, had good news judgment and explained what he wanted whenever he assigned a story. He also was patient if a story didn't quite hit the mark.

When Dan left to take a job at CNN International in Atlanta, a Brit named Chris Keeling moved into his spot. Chris was balding and somehow always managed to maintain a three-day growth of beard. His news judgment was good but unlike Dan he had no management skills.

Chris would assign a story by dropping a pile of wire copy on a writer's desk with the instruction, "Here, do this."

When asked how he wanted the story handled, he either didn't answer or would say, "Do whatever you want."

Invariably, when the piece was finished, his reaction would be, "Why did you do it like that?"

At least one rewrite would follow. Sometimes he did it himself.

Most of the editors were British and had been there for years. But recently hired writers were American. Presumably it dawned on RFE that it might be better for the news to have an American tilt since it was a U.S. radio station.

Old-timers said the staff had once been mostly Australian, some of whom drank beer at their desks.

There was no drinking in the newsroom anymore although two of the British editors were often a little looped when they returned from their breaks. Alcohol was served in the basement cafeteria which operated during the day Monday through Friday. Outside normal working hours, beer could be bought from vending machines.

Most of the editors had good news judgment and used only stories that merited coverage, but a few apparently thought they were being graded on story count, and they tried to make sure the in-house teletype never stopped.

One of them was Trevor Atkinson, a plump, balding, gap-toothed Englishman who looked as if his tractor was double-parked outside because he came to work in bib overalls. Trevor's main job was covering the morning/early afternoon shift on weekends. He always seemed to be putting out stories about what the Tamil Tigers were blowing up in their quest for an independent state in Sri Lanka – a topic I imagined generated little interest among East Europeans.

Management would periodically issue the results of in-house surveys in which the various desks would list story preferences. They always said they wanted more items from the United States and the European Union, especially stories about how the governments work. But the editors kept giving them the same old stuff.

Much to my disappointment, I eventually found myself working the slot frequently. I didn't care for the job because it was too hectic. What with clearing half a dozen teletypes that never seemed to stop, assigning stories, writing and editing copy, doing the top story list, there never seemed to be time for a break. As a writer, I could knock out a few stories, then get a cup of coffee and stretch my legs for a while.

On the day shift, Keeling would often take a full hour for lunch, moving me from writer to slot and leaving me in charge of the midday pandemonium. On weekends, the senior editor would almost always put me at the slot desk for the second half of my shift.

It was a real letdown when my name suddenly appeared on the schedule officially assigning me to the slot. Fortunately it didn't last long. My one and only full day in that job turned out to be my strangest experience ever in a newsroom.

My debut had me on the Sunday 2 to 10 shift with a gray-haired Scotsman named Roy Fairbain. The two of us would be taking over from Trevor, who had been there alone grinding out copy since 7 a.m.

When I walked in, Trevor relinquished the slot and stood around waiting for Roy to show up. As I started working, he asked if I had ever run the slot before. I foolishly told him the truth, that I had done it many times but that was my first time for a full eight hours.

Trevor paced around until Roy walked in a few minutes later. Then he said, "I worked through (my lunch break). I'm leaving now."

Roy responded by saying, "Well, I'm taking my break now."

He turned and left the room. It was rumored Roy had

some kind of a deal on the side to broadcast UK football scores on Sundays. That apparently was what he was doing.

As soon as Roy was through the door, Trevor went bonkers. His face turned bright red as he stomped around the room cursing in a loud voice, occasionally throwing pieces of paper in the air. I couldn't believe what I was seeing – a grown man throwing a preschool tantrum.

As I continued working, I tried to distract him a few times by asking his opinion on various news developments, but he ignored me. I didn't feel I had the authority to tell him to either shut up or leave the room.

Trevor continued ranting for a full half hour until Roy returned. Then he promptly departed.

Although I was astonished at what I had seen, I figured it was an aberration and didn't say anything to Roy. He went right to work and the rest of the shift was uneventful.

Another surprise awaited me the next day. As soon as I walked in, Terry Wiley, the news director who had succeeded Ken Thompson, cornered me and informed me I was off the slot because Trevor said I didn't know what I was doing!

I told her Trevor had some problem with Roy and hadn't paid the least bit of attention to me, so I couldn't understand why he would say such a thing. I suggested she ask Roy, Chris Keeling or any other editors about my abilities, but she abruptly ended the conversation by walking away.

I let the whole thing drop – for several reasons. One, I disliked the slot anyway and didn't want to talk my way back into it. Second, I liked "working through" myself so I could leave an hour early and I didn't want to be the one responsible for getting the practice banned. Third, I didn't want to get Roy in trouble.

I had always viewed Trevor as a buffoon and his ugly tirade cemented my opinion. I lost whatever respect I might have had for Wiley because, as a manager, she took drastic action without listening to both sides of the story.

Meanwhile, I continued working the slot unofficially

as if nothing had happened.

One of the things I really disliked about RFE was having to take the job home. Reading material, that is. In order to make sure no one missed anything, copies of every item on the NCA news wire were mass produced in the print shop and slipped into our IN boxes.

Whenever anyone returned from the weekend, there would be a stack of paper at least two inches thick to read. Some would toss the material straight into recycling bins but I always tried to read as much as I could. We had half an hour to catch up on our reading when we came in. If I had a lot to read and couldn't finish it, I took what was left home with me.

In addition to the news, we got copies of all the features and background pieces written by RFE reporters, plus newspaper clippings that might be useful. Those things were printed on salmon colored paper to differentiate them from the straight news on white paper. Of course, every single item made it into the burgeoning paper files.

Anyone who kept up with the reading material became a trivia expert on Eastern Europe. We knew all about Chechnya, Nagorno-Karabakh and other trouble spots long before most of the world ever heard of them.

The nicest thing about going on vacation was getting a break from the reading. It was a thrill to seal the opening to the IN box to stop the endless flow of paper.

Perhaps the greatest benefit of working at RFE was getting a military ID. A limited ID, however. We were given the IDs solely so we could play golf, go bowling or use other recreational facilities at U.S. military bases in Germany.

On the back of each card was a long list of what it was valid for. The good things like the commissary and PX were crossed off with a felt pen before the card was sealed in plastic. But that didn't stop some Americans, including me, from trying to get in anyway.

The commissaries were like big American supermarkets, stuffed with familiar products such as Cheerios, Oscar Meyer hot dogs and Tide detergent, all at very reasonable prices. They checked IDs at the entrance, so expulsion was painless. I either got in or I didn't. If I made it, it was like Christmas morning. I knew I could grab whatever I wanted and there wouldn't be any hassle.

The Army's convenience stores were a different story. Customers didn't have to show the card until they checked out. I'd flash mine at the cash register and hope the clerks didn't take a closer look. If they did, nothing could be more embarrassing. For the entertainment of the other people in line, I'd be told to get out, leaving my basket of goodies on the counter. But they always returned the card.

On a rare trip to Bonn to visit Chris Wright, I discovered the ID was honored at the little U.S. Embassy supermarket in Bad Godesberg, so Chris and I bought things like cookies and cereal. Perishable items were out for me because I had a six hour drive back to Munich.

One colleague – Gretel Johnston – resisted getting the ID for a long time, saying she had no desire to shop at the commissary. But her new Irish husband was a golfer. Since fees at German courses were high, she decided to get IDs for each of them, strictly for recreation.

Gretel may as well have hit the lotto. By chance, she was issued two cards valid for everything and they had no expiration date. She tried out the commissary once and couldn't resist stocking up regularly on staples such as steaks and Doritos, even though it was quite a drive. By that time, the only remaining U.S. military base in Munich had closed and she had to drive for nearly an hour to Augsburg.

Amazing Coincidence File: When I finished at Blue Danube Radio, a young Australian woman took over my job as well as my apartment. We became friends during the few days we knew each other.

Almost exactly one year later to the day, I took my first vacation at RFE, traveling with my sister Jane to Vienna and Budapest. While in Vienna, I stopped by Blue Danube to see if anyone I knew was still there. I learned the Australian woman was but she had just left for Budapest with a girlfriend. Several days later in Budapest, Jane and I were sitting in an out-of-the-way coffee house when the two of them walked in.

The unfortunate demise of Mr. Sluggo

In California, a few weeks before RFE notified me I'd been hired, Mr. Sluggo started throwing up. The first time was after he had eaten small pieces of baked potato skin. That was strange because he'd never had any problem before with potato skins.

After a few more incidents, I took him to the vet. His regular vet wasn't there that day, so a new, younger one saw us. She x-rayed him. Nothing unusual was found.

He continued throwing up. Not after every meal, but occasionally. The new vet suggested I get him castrated. I couldn't understand the connection between castration and vomiting even after she explained it, but I wanted to get the problem solved, so I agreed.

That didn't work.

The occasional vomiting continued even though he was eventually on a special diet of cottage cheese and home-made burgers made of rice and ground turkey. So it was back to the vet. This time she did an endoscopy. Once again, nothing unusual was found.

Between the castration and the endoscopy, Sluggo passed his 11th birthday, making him around 60 in human years. Despite his age, he was still frisky and enjoyed chasing a ball.

Suddenly it was time to leave for Germany. I didn't see any choice but to take him with me. I certainly couldn't leave him with my sister with instructions to get him cured. And I couldn't very well turn down the job because he was sick. After all, there were vets in Germany.

Once in Munich, Sluggo held up pretty well for the first few weeks but he was losing energy and weight. One reason for switching apartments was because the elevator stopped working a few times in the first building. Walking up and down six flights of stairs obviously would be too much for the dog, so I carried him. He was just under 20 pounds.

After moving to the new apartment, we saw a nearby vet. He suggested we go to the veterinary clinic at the University of Munich and get another endoscopy. The clinic was conveniently located right across the park from RFE.

That was a horrible experience. We literally had to wait a couple of hours in a crowded room full of barking dogs including several German Shepherds. Once in the examining room, I tried to explain the problem as half a dozen students in white coats leaned in to listen.

The next day I picked up Mr. Sluggo and got the standard report: nothing unusual was found. It was getting frustrating because he was still vomiting and losing weight.

I asked around at the office and the news director's secretary recommended a vet in a distant part of Munich. We went at night after work, taking a bus and two *Strassenbahnen*. After a brief wait, we saw the doctor, a woman. I explained what was happening and she handed me a few packets of Maalox. I was so discouraged I wanted to scream. I didn't, but I wish I hadn't paid her.

Back to the neighborhood vet. He performed a barium x-ray and reported seeing an obstruction in the duodenum, the connection between the stomach and the small intestine. He suggested exploratory surgery, saying, "If I can fix the problem, I will. If not, I'll put him to sleep."

That was too blunt for me. I asked around at the office again and two American guys recommended a vet with the appropriate name of Dr. Bohn. Fortunately, he had worked in the States and spoke English well. His office was on the north side of the city center, one bus and one *Strassenbahn* away from the apartment.

Dr. Bohn was an older man with thinning white hair.

He had a very soothing personality, sort of like the proverbial country doctor. By the time we saw him, Sluggo had lost a lot of weight. Dr. Bohn ruled out exploratory surgery, saying he was so weak he'd never survive it in any case.

He had a fluoroscope like those machines they had in shoe stores many years ago that made a green picture of the bones in the feet. He gave Sluggo some contrast solution, then put him under the fluoroscope. He let me watch. I could see the solution pulsing through his body. Once again, nothing unusual.

Dr. Bohn said the dog was fighting to stay alive and the best thing to do was to give him nourishment in the form of an infusion. He pulled out a plastic bag containing a clear liquid, probably half a liter. He connected it to a large needle, then injected the liquid under Sluggo's skin in several places. It was not pleasant to watch.

Sluggo's health continued declining. The doctor gave him two more infusions, each about 10 days apart. The end came one week after the third one, on January 25, 1991, when he died in the apartment. The details are better left unsaid.

I put Sluggo's body in a cardboard box and traveled to Dr. Bohn's office by taxi. The doctor was so curious about the cause of death that he offered to pay for an autopsy. He sent Sluggo's body to the veterinary school at Giessen, regarded as the best in Germany. I wondered how one ships a body, but didn't ask.

The autopsy showed the culprit was a tumor growing around Sluggo's small intestine. It encircled the intestine like a doughnut, constricting it to the width of a pencil. The growth couldn't be seen in the endoscopic exams because the scope probably didn't go that far. The small intestine is too wiggly to accommodate it.

I couldn't help feeling that the vets in California might have been able to find the tumor and save him if we hadn't moved to Germany. But who knows?

When I later explained the cause of death to his regular doctor in California, the one we hadn't seen, she said, "Oh, gee. We should have done exploratory surgery."

My biggest mistake of course was sticking with the new vet at the beginning and not insisting we see the regular one. But I never dreamed it was a life-or-death situation.

Introducing Mr. Dog

I was without a dog for nearly a year. I checked around in Germany for Shelties, but the breeders all seemed to be located far away in the middle of nowhere and I didn't want to rent a car to track them down.

Meanwhile, my sister Jane attended a Sheltie show, took photos of all the puppies and mailed them to me.

When I returned to her place for a visit in November of 1991, I phoned one of the breeders, a woman in a rural area near Los Gatos, south of San Francisco, and learned she had a six-week-old puppy for sale.

I drove there and it was love at first sight. Jumping around in a cardboard box in the corner of the kitchen was a cute little guy who was rejected as a show dog because he was expected to be too small. I like smaller Shelties anyway, so I immediately wrote a check as a deposit.

It was too soon for him to leave because he hadn't been weaned. I arranged to pick him up two weeks later, a couple of days before I was to fly back to Europe. I did so, then took him to the vet to be checked out. They asked what his name was. Not having given it any thought, I said Mr. Dog. He was in good condition except he needed routine treatment for worms.

A day or two later, we were out for a walk and I noticed him shivering despite the fact that it was sunny and warm. Back to the vet. He was diagnosed with a lung infection. He had to remain quiet for a week and take antibiotics. Going on the plane was forbidden.

Jane agreed to keep him until he was declared fit to travel. I flew back to Germany alone.

A week later, Mr. Dog's infection had been cured, but he immediately developed colitis and needed further treatment.

Finally, about two weeks after I had left, Jane and the puppy made the long drive across the bay to San Francisco International Airport only to learn that Lufthansa wouldn't take him. It was a classic Catch 22. Although the dog was too young for a rabies vaccination – they should be four months – the airline wouldn't ship him because he didn't have one.

I felt bad that Jane had gone to the airport for nothing. But it would have been a real disaster if the dog had traveled with me as planned. I would have had to miss my flight to get him back to Jane's place if he had been rejected. Of course I was foolish for not asking about dog importation before I left Germany, but I wasn't even sure I'd find one.

After scrambling around in Munich, I resolved the problem. For a small fee, I got a three-page certificate from the Bavarian Interior Ministry saying the dog could be admitted to Germany even though he hadn't been vaccinated. I faxed a copy to Jane so she could try again. This time I decided to use United Air Lines since Lufthansa had acted very German on the first attempt.

It worked. Mr. Dog arrived at the Munich airport at the age of three months, about one month after I had returned. But the fun wasn't over.

I reported to the United cargo area and was told the dog was there but they had lost the certificate. That was a shock, especially since I hadn't brought my copy. But I wanted to get the dog out of the box as soon as possible, so I went to customs anyway to see what I could do.

To my amazement, nothing was said about the missing certificate. Instead, the customs officer asked how much I paid for the dog and how much it had cost to ship him. He did some math on his calculator, then got out a large binder filled with columns of numbers.

He informed me I'd have to pay a tax of 98.82 DM

($62.84 at the time) because the dog was less than six months old. I asked what age had to do with it. He said a younger dog could very well be sold. In other words, he was a possible commodity.

I gladly paid, then returned to United. After a few minutes, they brought out the box from the back of the cargo area. The dog was obviously frightened and confused. He braced himself so well that I could hardly pry him out. But he quickly forgot about his terrifying journey after we found a nearby grassy area to walk in.

Mr. Dog was almost unrecognizable because he had practically doubled in size during the one month delay and looked more like a little fox than a fuzzy ball of fur.

A few days later, United found the missing certificate and mailed it to me even though it was totally useless at that point.

It snowed within a week. There were two to three inches on the ground. Although I was afraid the puppy might freeze his feet at his tender age, I took him out to experience the white stuff for the first time. He loved it, running around and scooping up snow with his nose.

It took me weeks to come up with a name for my new best friend. In looking over his family tree for ideas, I discovered one of his great grandparents was named My Buccaroo. The name certainly described his character, so I changed the spelling and he became Mr. Buckeroo. The standard spelling is buckaroo – a corruption of the Spanish word *vaquero,* which means cowboy.

Several months later, we visited the beach in Normandy. Buckeroo thought the sand was snow and plowed his nose into it. What a surprise!

After he reached the age of six months, I should have tried to get my 98 marks back, but it never occurred to me.

A solid offer

I maintained contact with Rendelsmann and was assigned two stories as a freelancer. I shot them on my days off, working with a photographer based in Augsberg.

One piece was for a monthly half hour program called *Focus on Europe.* The theme of that particular show was health care in Germany. My story dealt with how government health insurance covered doctor-prescribed visits to spas. We shot it in a small Bavarian town called Bad Wörishofen and I cut it at a studio north of Munich, within cycling distance of my apartment.

I learned there were about 260 locations where spa treatments were available and one out of every 10 Germans "took the cure" in his or her lifetime. One thing that made visiting a spa especially relaxing was the fact that German workers got paid leave while doing it.

The other story, for *European Journal,* was about the AFN (American Forces Network) radio station in Munich closing down after 46 years.

I was there when a German woman rushed into the studio to give the disc jockey a red rose after he announced it was the last broadcast. Unfortunately the camera wasn't rolling, and my ethics wouldn't let me stage it.

I interviewed a German TV personality visiting the station who got his start there in the 70s. He told me AFN was a positive influence on postwar generations in Germany, affecting the population's taste in music as well as the way news was presented.

EJ flew me to Cologne to edit that one. I had hoped to say hi to Rendelsmann but he wasn't in.

It might have been helpful if I had come up with a few story ideas on my own to keep me in the forefront of Rendelsmann's mind, but I hadn't given any thought to it.

In October of 1993, I received an unexpected call from Rendelsmann, who invited me to fly to the Cologne-Bonn airport to discuss a possible job. I flew there and we met for an hour in the coffee shop. He told me he'd like me to produce the show, saying, "I really want you for this job."

I said I was interested although I really wasn't because I preferred reporting.

I was belatedly starting to think about financial security. I was a little more than 18 months away from qualifying for a pension at RFE, and I'd never worked anywhere long enough to get one, so I asked Rendelsmann if they could include one. He said he'd get back to me.

A few weeks later, I flew to my sister's place in California for a two week vacation. I had almost forgotten about the conversation with Rendelsmann.

Hours after I arrived, in the middle of the night, a fax came in from him, waking me. It annoyed me that he waited until I was halfway around the world to get back in touch.

However, he did come up with a very good offer: a three-year contract at a salary of 9,675 DM per month ($5,972 at the time), plus moving expenses and a bonus if I completed the contract. It not only was an increase in marks, but it was worth a lot more in dollars because of the exchange rate. It took only 1.6 marks to buy a dollar in 1993 compared with 2.6 in 1983.

The only thing missing was a pension. The letter said they couldn't provide one. I had purposely raised the question to create an obstacle, but I probably would have jumped at the job if they had included one.

I sent Rendelsmann a fax asking if they could adjust the salary to compensate for giving up the RFE pension. As expected, he didn't respond and I didn't follow up.

Everything changed dramatically just a few weeks later in December when RFE announced it was going to close the Munich headquarters and establish a smaller office in Prague.

Special incentives were offered to encourage employees to quit. Everyone who left would be listed as terminated, and RFE regulations said anyone who was terminated would be credited with an extra year for pension purposes. That meant I'd only have to work for four years to get credit for five, and I'd qualify for the pension if I stayed through my anniversary date in early July, a little more than six months away.

After learning that, I wrote to Rendelsmann and told him I was thinking of leaving RFE. I asked if he still had an opening. His answer, to paraphrase, was, "No. Everything is fine. Couldn't be better."

In February, I wrote again, saying I was going to leave RFE for sure. I asked if there were any openings. I got the same answer.

Finally hired

I was amazed when I got a call a few weeks later from Sigfried Berndt, the head of *DW* television. I had met him soon after starting at the *Deutsche Welle* when he was in charge of North American Radio, and had run into him a few times since. I didn't know him well, but he seemed like a nice guy.

He said, "We want you to come back to Cologne and produce *European Journal*. Do you want to do it?"

I told him, "Yes, yes, of course."

He explained that the actual job of producer had been eliminated by the officials in Bonn. He said he'd give me a reporter's contract that had been turned down by a woman who preferred to freelance. He also wanted me to do occasional reporting. I said that would be fine – a big understatement.

The only problem, he said, was since the contract was for a reporter, it paid only 6,000 DM per month. I told him I'd been earning 7,000 when I left in 1988 and asked if he could match it. He said he'd get back to me.

I was so excited after I hung up that I was literally jumping up and down. I couldn't believe I had just been rehired shortly after getting a brushoff from Rendelsmann.

It was fantastic that everything had fallen into place. I would not only qualify for the RFE pension but I'd be going straight from one job to the other and wouldn't have to fool around applying for other jobs I didn't want.

Unfortunately, what followed might have made a good script for *I Love Lucy,* except it wasn't funny.

A few weeks later, Rendelsmann called and told me the salary would be 86,742 DM. I had no idea what that was per month, and I didn't have a calculator handy, so I asked him if I could have a few days to look at the number.

"OK," he said. "Take a few days, then send me your offer."

I hung up and figured it out: 7,228 DM. Not great, but at least they had topped my old salary. It didn't bother me that the pay was considerably less than what they had offered earlier. I didn't care how much they paid as long as I didn't have to take a cut. I wanted to get back to *EJ* and reporting, if only occasionally, and that was probably my last chance.

Since Rendelsmann had asked me to make an offer, I considered various ways of coming up with a figure, such as checking the inflation rate since I had left and asking for a cost of living increase. But in the end I decided he had really put me on the spot. It was too dangerous to ask for a specific number because if it wasn't what he wanted to hear, the whole thing would collapse.

The best way to handle it was to leave it up to him. Two days after our conversation, I sent him a letter asking if he could "move the salary in the direction of the October offer of 9,675 DM."

About a week later, while awaiting a reply, I got a surprise call from Peter Morello.

He asked, "How's it going with Rendelsmann?"

"Fine. We're just a hair away from settling everything. I expect to hear from him in a day or two."

Apparently he wasn't listening. He said, "Well, I'm the chairman of the search committee. You know, there are two other Americans who want that job."

"Oh?"

"There's a guy in Frankfurt and a woman in Rome."

"Does either one have any producing experience?"

"No, but the guy was a reporter in Denver."

I thought, "So what? They need a producer."

"You know," he said, "They're not going to pay more than 6,000."

"Oh, that's good to know."

He wrapped up the conversation by saying, "Look, I really want to see you back here. If there's anything I can do to help, let me know."

After I hung up, I wondered what he was up to. I assumed he was just snooping around, trying to find out what my salary was. I couldn't believe that, as "chairman of the search committee," he didn't know the job had been filled.

Actually, it wouldn't have hurt to have told him I already had the job, but clamming up was an automatic reflex with Peter.

One thing was certain: something crazy was going on. I decided to phone Rendelsmann instead of waiting for him to get back to me. I started calling the following Monday, trying three times during the day. His secretary told me he was either in a meeting, on another line or out of the office.

I didn't have an answering machine, so except for very brief dog walks, I stayed in the apartment the whole day waiting for his call. I kept thinking, "Filling this job has to be one of the most important things he has to do. Why won't he get back to me?"

On Tuesday, I continued trying. Finally, on the third attempt, Rendelsmann himself answered with his customary growl.

"Hi, it's Walt Christophersen."

"I'm pissed off."

"What?"

"I'm pissed off because you're trying to bargain."

I thought, "You fool, I'm not trying to bargain. You asked me to make a counter-offer, and I didn't even do that."

Instead I said, "You mean the salary is non-negotiable? It's *fest?*"

"Yes."

"Well that's OK. It's OK. It's ... O ... K."

I knew I had to really nail down the job. Without thinking I said: "Let's set a starting date. My last day at Radio Free Europe is the 5th of July. How about the middle of the month? What day of the week is the 15th?"

I heard him shuffle some papers. Then he said, "It's a Friday."

"Is it OK with you if I start on a Friday?"

"Yes."

"All right," I said, very deliberately, "I will start ... at *European Journal* ... on Friday ... the 15th ... of July. OK?"

"OK."

There was a brief pause. Then he said: "You're not just looking for a desk job, are you?"

I said, "No. Of course not," thinking, "What kind of a goofy question is that?"

We said goodbye.

After I hung up, I thought, "Whew, that was close. He's so crazy I almost lost the job."

I knew there was something else we should have discussed, but it didn't hit me until two days later. "Christ," I thought, "I have to get the salary in writing before he changes his mind."

On Friday, I sent him a letter which said: "Could you do me a favor and put the salary in writing so there won't be any misunderstandings later on?"

I suggested he list whatever benefits there might be, such as moving expenses and other things he had offered in October. I said I'd be in France the following week, and if he could send his letter in the meantime, I'd phone him when I got back so we could finalize everything.

Putting the agreement in writing was standard procedure at *European Journal,* but in view of the trouble Mary Beth, Peter and I had getting paid at the beginning, I didn't want to take any chances.

Actually I didn't care whether they paid moving expenses or not. If they did, it would count as extra income. If I paid, it would be a tax writeoff, so I probably would have been better off handling it myself. But I figured the company would automatically pay for a move within Germany.

I didn't have to worry about my eventual return to the United States because RFE would buy my plane ticket and cover the shipment of my personal effects no matter when I left. The only thing I'd have to pay for was shipping the dog.

When I got back from France, I rushed to the mailbox. There was nothing from the *Deutsche Welle*. I had an ominous feeling. I convinced myself not to get excited, that I should wait a few days before phoning him. I figured he'd say, "Look, I'm very busy. Don't worry, you'll get it. Just don't press me."

Once in the past, Rendelsmann had chastised me for pushing too hard to get rehired. Knowing how irrational and unpredictable he could be, I didn't want to risk antagonizing him.

By Wednesday, April 27th, I was getting concerned. I remembered the call from Morello and decided maybe he could do some checking for me. If Peter hadn't phoned in the first place, I never would have thought of contacting him. I didn't want to phone him because I knew he would ask what my salary was and I didn't want to tell him it was none of his business. So I wrote:

> "What the hell is going on up there? I've been trying to get Rendelsmann to put the salary in writing and he won't do it. As you know from our past experience, there's no way I can move to Cologne without having the deal in writing.

You said you want to help me get back there.
Do me a favor and find out what the delay is."

There was no immediate response, so a few days later I sent Rendelsmann a brief note: "I'm still waiting for the salary in writing. Is there a problem?"
A week later, I sent the same note again.

The unraveling

On May 10, a letter in a *Deutsche Welle* envelope turned up in the mail box. I was relieved. As I took the elevator to my floor, I held up the envelope and said, "Finally. Finally. I finally have it."
Then I thought, "I'm almost afraid to open it. It could be something totally wacko."
I set the letter down on the kitchen table and tried to ignore it, but couldn't.
I was right. It was totally wacko.
Writing in English, Rendelsmann said:

> "I am rather put out by the fact that you seem inclined to see the work in terms of a 'desk job' than as in-the-field reporting. While no one disputes the value of an experienced producer, the fact remains that my needs are better served, given the current climate, by having a flexible reporter in the team.
> "I am currently involved in negotiations with an excellent young reporter, whose abilities are such that he will no doubt be capable of working as a producer as well."

I said to myself, "Oh, come on, don't be ridiculous." It looked like a new version of, "Be patient. There are other candidates." Except, unlike the last time, we had a solid agreement.

Rendelsmann also wrote, "My hands are more or less tied as far as the salary is concerned."

My thinking on that was, "Yeah, I know. We've already been through that. Let's move on."

It was ironic that Rendelsmann had everything backwards. Despite all the mistakes I had made, like leaving Cologne after my second contract ran out, he was giving me exactly what I wanted when he changed the emphasis to reporting. After five and a half years of trying to convince him to rehire me as a reporter, I couldn't imagine where he got the idea I no longer wanted to do it. Whenever the subject of producing came up, it was they who initiated it. I never once independently expressed any interest in producing.

I felt like getting Rendelsmann on the phone and telling him, "Stop this idiocy."

But I reminded myself, "No. you have to be diplomatic."

So I wrote:

> "There's no reason for you to be concerned about me working as a reporter. If you check the files, you'll find I produced more stories on average than any other reporter who ever worked there, and I haven't changed. I know most of the people there and get along with them fine. I know how everything is done and could start at full speed on the first day. I don't know how you could even think of hiring an outsider."

I didn't mention the salary because I couldn't figure out why he had brought it up again. It looked like much ado about nothing, Rendelsmann being Rendelsmann.

After getting no immediate response, I sent another note. I thought that would be better than phoning because he'd have something he could refer to, unless he threw it out. Plus,

I was still annoyed about having to waste two days earlier trying to get in touch with him by phone.

I wrote:

> "I don't know what's going on, but I want to get this thing settled as soon as possible. I have to start packing, and I don't even know if I'm going to Cologne or California. I suggest I come to Cologne so we can meet face-to-face and work out whatever the problem is."

Once again, no reply. Since my starting date was little more than six weeks away, I decided to rent a car, drive to Cologne and demand that he put the agreement in writing.

I made arrangements with a small company that started weekend rentals at noon on Thursday. I'd drive to Cologne, stay in a hotel near the *Deutsche Welle*, then drop in on Rendelsmann Friday morning to get everything cleared up. Saturday morning I'd look for an apartment.

Two days before I was scheduled to pick up the car, a letter arrived from Rendelsmann. I was shocked.

Writing in German this time, he said:

> "As I said in my last letter, there's nothing more I can do for you at this time. We've decided to hire another candidate. His salary requirements match ours. I have the feeling he eventually could develop into a a good producer. Have a nice time in California."

I yelled, "Rendelsmann, you son of a bitch!"

Of course his previous letter hadn't said, "There's nothing more I can do for you." If it had, I would have phoned him immediately.

Apparently when he wrote that he was talking to

someone else, that was his strange way of telling me I'd been fired. But it didn't register.

His use of the words "another candidate" irked me. I hadn't realized I'd been demoted from employee.

I assumed the reference to the salary meant he had found someone who would work for 6,000 DM. My salary certainly met their "requirements." It was their offer.

The last line was especially cruel: "Have a nice time in California." But I had unwittingly invited it by suggesting an alternative to Cologne.

I was amazed that he was so mercenary that he could jettison a reporter he knew to be dedicated and hard-working and replace him with a total stranger simply to save money.

I picked up the rental car anyway and drove south to the winter resort area of Garmisch-Partenkirchen where Buckeroo and I spent a few hours walking the mountain trails as I tried to clear my head.

I figured Rendelsmann got what he wanted and there was no way I could change it. Besides, I intended to keep trying and didn't want to burn any bridges. So I sent him a letter saying I still wanted the job very much. I asked him to keep me in mind if the new guy didn't work out.

I put my things in storage again and regretfully returned to California in August of 1994. I had considered moving to Cologne to beg for freelance work but I wanted the security of a contract and I figured it would be too tough on my ego to be bumping into my replacement.

I was able to keep up with *European Journal* because it was broadcast on a PBS station in San Mateo, south of San Francisco. When I saw my replacement, I didn't care for him. But of course I was terribly biased.

After a few weeks in California, I sent Rendelsmann a letter saying I was very upset that he had dropped me. To make sure he understood everything, I again hired a young German attending UC Berkeley to translate the letter. I said as far as I was concerned, the next contract was mine, and since we already had a salary, all we had to do was set a new starting date. I told him it wouldn't cost anything to get me there because my household articles were in storage in Germany and I would gladly pay my own plane fare.

He replied quickly this time, in German, saying, "Until I received your letter, I hadn't realized what a basic misunderstanding we had."

A misunderstanding? About what? I had no idea what he was talking about. I almost wished he hadn't said anything, preferring to continue believing he had dumped me to save money rather than learn I apparently had been fired by mistake.

Rendelsmann said all he could offer me was a *Prognose* (temporary job) that paid 36,000 DM, adding, "You couldn't live on that." He told me he'd let me know if anything else came up. Meanwhile, he said contacting him again would be "a waste of energy and time."

A short while later, I received a surprise fax from Morello. I didn't even know how he knew where I was. He said he hadn't seen my letter until August because he'd been traveling for six weeks. But four months had passed since I sent my letter from Munich to Cologne.

What he said was astonishing:

> "The contract offer was a missed opportunity. A few days after we spoke, Rendelsmann told me he had received a letter from you stating 10,600 per month. He said it was too high, and he would inform you of that. He also told me to continue the search as you were no longer a candidate."

Of course I hadn't sent any such letter. The closest Rendelsmann ever got to mentioning a salary dispute was his odd reference to his hands being tied. No one in his right mind would have asked for a 50% increase, especially after being told the salary was non-negotiable.

I responded to Peter's fax by saying the demand for 10,600 DM was "pure fantasy." I told him I had accepted an offer of a little more than 7,000 and was very angry that he hadn't told me what Rendelsmann was up to.

Although I was very annoyed with Peter, I was curious about how much they had paid my replacement, so I sent him a fax later and asked. The answer was 6,250 DM – roughly 1,000 less than my new salary. Peter also listed the salaries of everyone else in the office. That's why I didn't tell him anything when he called in Germany. He would have told everyone in the building what I would have been earning.

The whole debacle was incredible considering I had known Rendelsmann for more than 10 years and worked with him for five. I had occasionally attended small parties at his house in addition to seeing him in connection with his dog-sitting duties. His wife even took my sister shopping once.

I'm tempted to use the word stupid to describe how I mishandled the whole affair, but I like to think it was more a case of being naive. It never occurred to me that he might dump me. I considered myself part of the family.

The big mystery was whether Rendelsmann had purposely made up the story about the salary dispute or was hallucinating. I could understand him making it up, but there's no way I could comprehend him believing a letter had materialized out of thin air.

It would be an oversimplification to say he was crazy. But I wouldn't be surprised if he had attention deficit disorder. At least five percent of school-aged children in the United States are said to be affected by it, and half never outgrow it. People with ADD are usually inattentive, easily distracted and impulsive. That certainly described Rendelsmann. When I told him the salary was OK, it's possible it went in one ear and out the other, and when he hung up he had no recollection that we had an agreement. A dose of Ritalin might have changed everything.

Another possibility is that he suspected the *Deutsche Welle* wanted to get rid of him, and he believed he could impress his bosses by saving money. The easiest way to do that was to dump me and hire someone who would work for the original salary.

I wondered if I was the only one Rendelsmann treated so badly. Apparently not. When I told my friend Ulla he had dumped me, she said, *"Ja, typisch* (typical) *Rendelsmann."*

It was also Ulla who once said, "Out of sight, out of mind." Meaning, "Out of Cologne, out of luck."

When I wrote to Mary Beth, she suggested that cultural differences may have played a part. At first I laughed. But after I thought about it, I realized she might have a point. It wasn't so much cultural differences as the fact that I had tried to be very respectful and diplomatic in order to compensate for whatever differences there might be.

This ... is CNN

With *European Journal* at least temporarily out of the picture, I lined up two job interviews. First, I drove to Medford, Oregon, to discuss the possibility of working as a news director, then flew to Atlanta to talk to CNN. I had originally written to CNN International but my letter was passed on to CNN domestic. I figured if I got hired there, I'd try to get transferred to CNNI.

At CNN, I met with Kim Engebretsen, whose title was chief copy editor. As I took the dreaded writing test, she checked one of my references, then offered me a job on the spot. I asked if I could have a few days to think about it. When I got back to California, I phoned Medford to see what my status was. The GM said she wanted me to return for a second interview. Figuring a bird in hand is better than two in the bush, I decided to go with CNN.

I had paid my own plane fare to get to Atlanta because Engebretsen had said she would see me if I "happened to turn up." But after she hired me, they reimbursed me.

I drove to Atlanta and started work in December of 1994. Fortunately CNN paid to put me in a hotel for an entire month. Unfortunately I never had a worse time finding a place to live. I had hoped to rent a house on the north side of the city, but every rental I looked at was in shabby condition. Just before the month was up, I got desperate and took an apartment in a big complex I didn't like. I was 11½ miles from CNN, a 20 minute drive outside the rush hour.

It was nice to get my furniture out of the warehouse in Ohio, where it had been for nearly 12 years. It was even nicer that CNN paid the shipping costs.

RFE sent my personal effects over from Munich, so I had everything together for a change.

I worked in that big room behind the anchor desk that everyone could see on TV. As usual, it was tough being the new guy, and that was made worse by two copy editors who seemed to enjoy nit-picking my work. Unlike the casual atmosphere at RFE, there were strict deadlines and we were almost always racing the clock to get everything done.

Most of the writers and producers were in their 20s and 30s. When Burl Ives died in April, 1995, younger staffers said they'd never heard of him, even though he was a folk singer with more than 40 albums to his credit and radio stations were still playing his recording of "Holly Jolly Christmas" every year. He had also won an Academy Award for Best Supporting Actor for *The Big Country* (1958) and played Big Daddy in the film *Cat on a Hot Tin Roof* (1958).

On the other hand, many of the older staffers including me had never heard of the singer Selena until she was murdered. It's a good thing more than one generation was represented in the newsroom.

The work schedules varied, but most of the time I was

on a shift that started at 7 p.m. There usually were four writers. We would have the first hour to read up on the news. We got together for a planning session at 8, where the producer would hand out the rundown for the hour-long 10 p.m. show. The writers would bid on stories they wanted, each winding up with several. After the 10 was written, we worked on at least two later half hour newscasts.

The worst shift was one that started later in the evening and ended at 5:30 a.m. One writer got stuck with that shift so he or she could write a five minute newscast airing at 5.

I was working that shift on April 19, 1995, the day the federal building in Oklahoma City was destroyed by a bomb. It was not only my toughest day at CNN, but the most frantic day I ever had in TV news.

Because it was such a momentous story, management decided to do a fresh hour-long newscast every hour throughout the night. That decision, I later learned, was made at 10:30 p.m. Because of the late hour, it was also decided that it was too late to call in extra writers. So the four of us who were already there had to write a new show every hour until 5 a.m. when the morning shift was ready to go.

Although there was a lot of recycling for each show, writing a fresh newscast every hour with only four people was nearly impossible. But somehow we did it, finishing each show more than halfway through, then starting on the next one. Normally we'd be running around checking tapes we hadn't seen to make sure everything was OK. But there wasn't time for that. Jumping up to run to the washroom or get something to drink seemed almost sinful. Everyone who walked out of there at 5 a.m. must have been as shell-shocked as I was.

I was surprised everything had to be scripted. I expected CNN to handle the bombing the same as KPIX covered the earthquake, with everything improvised. Someone speculated later that maybe management hadn't trusted the anchor to ad-lib. But the whole night was such a blur, I didn't know who the anchor was, or remember anyone else who was there.

I often wondered what would happen if all the computers crashed at the same time. I found out while we were preparing a Sunday evening newscast.

Individual computers went out once in a while. Someone from the tech staff would eventually show up to get them going again. But that time all the computer screens were blank. And they stayed blank.

It was about 25 minutes before the hour. Suddenly, from a back room somewhere, producers and interns hauled out a bunch of dinosaur electric typewriters. We were told to rewrite whatever we had done earlier on prompter paper, from memory, as fast as we could. Amazingly, everyone did it and the show went on with no apparent problems. The computers came back a little while later.

Red-Eye to Berlin

I hadn't lost interest in returning to Germany. I was even able to keep up with *European Journal* because one of the two Atlanta PBS stations carried it.

After Germany was reunified, there was a dramatic change in the status of the *Deutsche Welle*. It was merged with a Berlin radio station known as RIAS (Radio in the American Sector), which had been founded by the U.S. government in 1946 to provide propaganda-free news for the city.

The plan was to incorporate RIAS into the German broadcasting system. It was thought the *Deutsche Welle* would absorb the much smaller radio station, but RIAS pulled off an amazing coup and took over the *Welle* on May 1, 1992.

The new administration was determined to get rid of *European Journal* and move all television production to Berlin. Learning there might be opportunities there, I wrote to Christoph Lanz, the TV chief, in April of 1995 and asked if he needed any reporters.

A guy named Patrick McGee phoned a short time later and asked me to FedEx my tape. I did. McGee phoned again and said they were interested in me as an anchor. They wanted me in Berlin as soon as possible to do an audition. I hadn't thought much about anchoring, but it sounded like a great opportunity.

A few days later, only five months after I had started at CNN, I was in Berlin, having slipped away during my Monday-Tuesday weekend. I went directly to an expensive hotel they provided and tried to wake up by splashing around in the shower. Then I shaved, got into my suit and took a taxi to the *Deutsche Welle*, located in a huge onetime factory building just inside the former East Berlin.

I met McGee, a large casually dressed guy with short hair who was something of a geek. Then I did the audition, reading the script from the previous newscast. I had no idea how good or bad I was. I hadn't read aloud for years and was groggy from lack of sleep. I never did meet Lanz, only McGee and Herr Bruggemann, a bureaucrat in a suit who worked under Lanz.

Less than 24 hours after arriving in Berlin, I was on my way back to Atlanta. I've never been able to sleep on a plane, so I was dead tired. I got back to my apartment by mid-afternoon, picked up Buckeroo at a nearby vet, took him for a walk, got cleaned up, then arrived at CNN at 7 p.m. to work my regular shift. I was totally spaced out until midnight.

The *Deutsche Welle* reimbursed me for my plane ticket, which was well over $1,000 because it was purchased on short notice.

Some weeks later, I received a letter from Bruggemann saying thanks but they didn't want me. I was naturally disappointed, so I wrote to Lanz and asked if he could provide any details on what was wrong with my audition. His answer came in July. It was quite a surprise:

> "We were impressed and satisfied with your on-screen presence and would have liked to hire you. However, a thorough knowledge

of German has proven to be necessary for the anchors of our English and Spanish news shows. Mr. McGee and Mr. Bruggemann have told me that, unfortunately, your German skills do not meet our requirements."

Although I never claimed to be a linguist, I felt cheated. I wrote to Lanz and pointed out that I had had a 20 minute conversation in German with Bruggemann and there were no communication problems. I said since I had never met him (Lanz), I'd like to see him personally so he could judge for himself if my German was good enough. (I might have scored big points by sending my letter in German, but I hadn't thought of it.)

Lanz replied quickly, saying he'd be glad to see me the next time I got to Germany. Over the next six months, I took two consecutive German courses at the Atlanta branch of the Goethe Institute. One class was on Saturday morning and it was tough getting up after only three hours sleep. Despite that, I was the only student with a perfect attendance record. I didn't learn much, but it helped keep the German fresh in my mind.

I kept Rendelsmann apprised of my whereabouts in case a miracle happened and he came up with a job for me. Just weeks after I returned from Berlin, I received a letter from him in which said he was about to be ousted. Instead of being nasty like his previous letter, this one was sad:

"After 30 years with the *Deutsche Welle*, I'm giving up my job to devote myself to the 'pleasures' of early retirement. Leaving doesn't come easily to me, but the structural changes that have come with *Deutsche Welle* TV leave me no option. I fear *European Journal* is going to die."

Rendelsmann himself died eight months later, in February of 1996. The official cause of death was kidney cancer. But it's said he really died of a broken heart because the *Deutsche Welle* had dumped him. I never got a chance to tell him I knew exactly how he felt.

European Journal as I had known it ceased to exist in April when it became a rehash of stories from German TV with no original reporting. The program was moved out of the studio, presumably to cut expenses, and a British anchorman was taped in the streets of Brussels introducing the stories. Instead of using American narrators, the pieces were voiced by English-speaking Germans.

As *European Journal* faded into obscurity, the real tragedy was that the program never realized its enormous potential because the folks in charge had never understood what a great thing they had.

With all the resources at the program's disposal, it could have been considerably better. One thing we kept harping on was the need for an experienced American producer. The pay was good enough to attract a talented person from the United States but when they finally got around to taking our advice, they hired the first guy who walked through the door.

The big bosses never figured out the best way to keep the show on the air was to make it too good to cancel.

Jumping to CNNI

After more than one year at CNN domestic, I managed to make the switch to CNN International. Dan Williams, who had worked at RFE in Munich, was still there. He may have put in a good word for me.

My new boss was Ted Iliff, a burly, good-natured man with round glasses and a handlebar mustache. He had been at RFE some years before I was, and indicated he thought anyone who worked there was automatically OK. He hadn't been in charge when I first applied to CNNI. If he had, I probably could have skipped CNN domestic.

He gave me a sizable salary increase, saying he wanted me to work as a copy editor. That didn't appeal to me, but I was so eager to get out of domestic, I took the job anyway.

CNNI was on a lower floor, but the layout was similar, with the writers' desks forming the backdrop behind the anchor. After putting in a few months as a writer, I was eased into an editor's chair and I was surprised to find I enjoyed it.

The editors not only had to make sure the scripts were accurate, they had to tell the story concisely and be easy to read aloud. We also had to verify that the correct video and fonts were used and they all had the proper numbers that the director used to get them on the screen.

Other responsibilities included making sure the writers followed CNN style, such as spelling adviser with an "e" instead of an "o," writing Muslim not Moslem and saying African-American instead of black.

Having experienced nit-picking from two copy editors while I was at CNN domestic, I was more tolerant of the writers than I might have been. If a story made sense, I would approve it rather than trying to rewrite everything in my style. If a story needed reworking, Iliff encouraged us to discuss it with the writer, time permitting, so he or she could touch it up and learn from the experience.

I was on the overnight shift, 9:30 p.m. to 7:30 a.m. Yes, 10 hours. But we only worked four days a week. That was Iliff's idea, imported from RFE, where the overnight editors were on the same schedule.

One benefit of working the overnight was getting an extra 10% on our paycheck. Another was that there were fewer bosses to contend with.

The major disadvantage was a chronic lack of sleep that turned most of us into zombies. Talking with other staffers, I learned I wasn't the only one who hung a black sheet over his bedroom window to try to shut out the daylight. But despite the sheet, I always woke up after only five hours and was rarely able to get back to sleep. I happened to read an article that said a five hour limit on sleep was common among overnight workers. Colleagues I questioned said they had the same experience. One of the editors claimed he avoided chronic fatigue by maintaining the same schedule seven days a week. I couldn't see staying up all night on my days off.

    CNNI produced a fresh 30 minute newscast at the top of each hour. Pre-taped programs ran at the half hour.

    There were always two copy editors. We would alternate shows, one taking midnight, 2 and 4 a.m. and the other taking the odd hours. We each kept an eye on our newscast until it was over, then after a brief break we started editing the next one as the stories filtered in.

    On nights when we had an extra person, one of the supervising producers would occasionally ask me to write and voice a package. It was nice to keep my hand in that part of the business.

    The work was routine except for occasional live shots from the Middle East after something blew up. The normal routine went out the window on Saturday night and Sunday morning, August 30 and 31, 1997 – the night Princess Diana was killed in a car crash in Paris.

    The story was breaking as I went to work and I knew it would be a frantic evening. I was right. Virtually the entire CNNI staff was immediately sent upstairs to CNN domestic to help out on Princess Di coverage. Perhaps management had learned a lesson from understaffing following the Oklahoma City bombing. The newsroom was crawling with people.

    I was assigned to write and supervise the editing of a profile of Diana's boyfriend, Dodi Al-Fayed, assisted by interns who gathered file footage. That took about an hour and a half. After that, I had nothing to do until returning to CNNI just before it was time to leave.

    Getting breaking news on is always a perilous situation because so many things can go wrong, but it's something that has to be done. I was amazed at how the CNN directors could consistently keep the show flowing smoothly when everything was being improvised.

Berlin epilogue

I got back to Germany in May of 1996 and went to Berlin again. I finally met Lanz, a very personable guy who was young and thin, dressed in a dark shirt and tie with jeans. Sitting in his office, joined by Bruggemann, we discussed a possible anchor job. Lanz alternated between English and German, speaking German when he hit a rough spot in English.

The job sounded terrific – 10,000 DM ($6,535) to work for one week a month anchoring a daily newscast called *Journal*. I could live literally anywhere in the world and fly to Berlin once a month to work. I was amazed when Lanz said he was "impressed" with my German, noting that McGee, the native English speaker, had told him I spoke no German whatsoever.

Lanz invited me to return the next morning for another audition. I did, and felt it went better than the first time, mainly because I'd been in Germany for a few days and didn't have jet lag.

But Lanz apparently didn't share that feeling. At an afternoon meeting, he offered to hire me as a copy editor with the "possibility" of anchoring sometime in the future. The pay would be 9,000 per month. He asked me to think about it on my flight back.

I was tempted to ask what happened to my fabulous "on-screen presence" but I didn't want to put him on the spot.

I wasn't thrilled at being instantly downgraded from 10,000 DM for one week to 9,000 for four weeks. And I certainly wasn't interested in working as a copy editor anyway.

Back in Atlanta, I sent Lanz a letter thanking him for the audition but declined his offer. They later reimbursed me for my plane fare. I felt a little guilty about taking their money because I had spent an entire week in Germany, but not guilty enough to refuse it.

It was becoming clear that a return to the *Deutsche*

Welle was not in the cards. I tried two more times in the next couple of years to get something going in Berlin, but all I got was an invitation to visit the city at my own expense to take a "translator assessment test." *Nein, danke.*

    CNN always listed dozens of job openings in the computer. I kept applying for anything that offered more variety, but nothing developed. I eventually quit to see if I could find a way to earn a living without going to an office every day. Maybe write a book?

    It's ironic that the best job I ever had had a time limit. Rather than be bitter about failing to reconnect in Cologne, I've tried to focus on how incredibly lucky I was to have lived and worked as a European – something I'd never imagined.

    Although every day was a new adventure, I'll never forget the great times exploring the hallowed beaches of Normandy, the grandeur of Mont St. Michel and the tragedy of Oradour, encountering fascinating people such as Donald Jones, Howard Gillingham and Dame Jean Conan Doyle, and learning more about everything from Vincent van Gogh to the little Belgian town that was saved by gingerbread cookies.

    To borrow a modern cliché, it was a great ride.

Who was that masked man?

Walt Christophersen has been a professional writer for decades, working primarily in television news.

His most recent full time job was with CNN International in Atlanta, where he served as a copy editor, making sure scripts for worldwide broadcast were clear, concise, accurate and easy-to-read.

He arrived at CNN from Munich, where he had been a writer/editor for Radio Free Europe, the Cold War radio station that sent unadulterated news to the former Soviet Union and Eastern Europe.

Before that, he worked as a reporter for *European Journal*, the weekly TV newsmagazine based in Germany which formed the basis for this book.

Like many people in TV news, Christophersen held almost every job there is in a newsroom: writer, reporter, producer, assignment editor and video photographer/editor, plus running the whole shop as news director.

He got into journalism in college when a friend became editor of the campus newspaper at the University of the Pacific in Stockton, California. He told the friend, "Hey, I think it would be fun to write a column." The friend said, "OK. Do it."

What resulted was a Herb Caen-type column* that was the first thing many students turned to when the paper came out. Those columns proved to be more useful than he ever dreamed. When Christophersen was interviewed for his first TV job as a newswriter at WBBM (CBS) in Chicago, he took them along as writing samples. After the news director hired him, he told Christophersen one reason he got the job was because he enjoyed reading the columns.

* Caen was a true legend who wrote for decades for the *San Francisco Chronicle*. He might be described as a whatever-pops-into-my-head columnist.

Other TV work followed in San Diego, Burbank and San Francisco, plus Greenville, North Carolina and Columbus, Ohio.

Getting into reporting was partly by chance. As news director in Greenville, he occasionally had to cover stories due to staff shortages. That led to shooting stories on Sundays with the chief photographer to punch up the usually light Monday newscasts as well as pocket extra money by selling the pieces to the CBS afternoon feed, which sent secondary network stories and affiliate contributions to stations all over the country.

Without those stories, there would have been no audition tape and no work on *European Journal*.

Christophersen took breaks several times over the years and went off to see the world, visiting more than 100 countries and dozens of Pacific islands. He spent a number of years contributing freelance travel articles to major newspapers such as the *Chicago Tribune, Los Angeles Times, San Francisco Examiner, Boston Globe* and *Toronto Star*.

In addition to his broadcast work, he served as press secretary in Washington, DC for Congressman David Towell of Nevada, a friend who served for one term in the early 70s.

All quotes in this book are real, not made up or recreated. Statements made by people interviewed for stories were taken from transcripts. Everyday conversations quoted were burned into my brain.   W.C.

www.ingramcontent.com/pod-product-compliance
Lightning Source LLC
Chambersburg PA
CBHW031551300426
44111CB00006BA/270